State Fair Carousel

Saving a Minnesota Treasure

Nancy Peterson and Peter Boehm

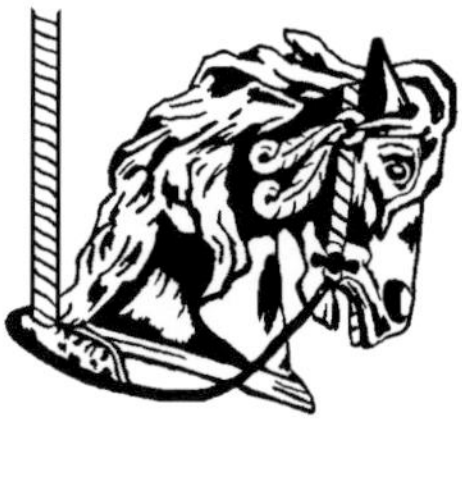

Published by Our Fair Carousel, Inc.
Owner and operator of Cafesjian's Carousel

Photos not otherwise identified as to source or photographer were taken by Nancy Peterson

Cover design: Nancy Peterson
Text design: Peter Boehm

Our Fair Carousel, Inc.
1245 Midway Parkway
Saint Paul, MN 55103
www.OurFairCarousel.org

Contents

For Augie and Vi
and grandchildren everywhere

with thanks to all
who have helped care for
PTC 33 / the State Fair Carousel /
now Cafesjian's Carousel,
including more than 1,000 volunteers
whose names are displayed
at Cafesjian's Carousel
in Saint Paul's Como Park

Preface: A Minnesota Treasure

Once upon a time, a wonderful carousel was built for the people of Minnesota. It arrived at the State Fair in 1914 and became a family tradition for generations of city dwellers and outstate visitors alike. In 1988, just before the carousel's 75th birthday, Minnesotans were shocked to learn that the carousel had been dismantled and 20 of its 68 horses were on their way to New York to be auctioned to collectors.

This book is the story of this very special Minnesota carousel, known in the carousel world as PTC33, and how it was almost lost forever. More important, it tells how the people of Minnesota came together to save a valued old treasure. How do we know about this? Because for 25 years we've been at the center of the massive volunteer effort to save, restore, house, and operate the carousel. We have met a lot of heroes along the way, including more than 1,000 people who have helped and one remarkably generous donor — Jerry Cafesjian — for whom the carousel is now named. Meanwhile, the carousel has emerged as a jewel of the community and a favorite among carousel fanciers across the nation and around the world.

We are writing this book to celebrate the carousel's 100th birthday and to recognize the great community-wide spirit that has kept it spinning.

We are also telling the story for the next generation of riders, volunteers, donors, and leaders, because *you* will write the next chapter in the life of this Minnesota treasure.

— Nancy Peterson and Peter Boehm

Peter Boehm and Nancy Peterson are co-founders of the nonprofit Our Fair Carousel, Inc., caretaker of Cafesjian's Carousel.

1

Minnesota's Fair Carousel

When you consider that about 6,000 wooden carousels were built in the United States between 1895 and 1930, and that fewer than 170 still operate, you can understand how fortunate we Minnesotans are that one of those survivors is alive and well and, as we write this, in St. Paul's Como Park celebrating its 100th birthday.

The 5,830 carousels that did not survive? They were lost to flood and fire, or abandoned, or broken up and sold at auction. Any of these things could have happened to the Minnesota state fair carousel, now known as Cafesjian's Carousel. In 1939, for example, a section of the carousel building was in flames; only some very smart fire-fighting prevented the carousel's total destruction. In the 1940s when the carousel didn't produce much revenue an owner could have hauled it to a junkyard. In 1988 the horses came within minutes of being sold piecemeal at auction. Instead, in the hands of volunteers, the carousel took on a whole new life.

Cafesjian's Carousel is not merely a survivor, it is a stellar carousel. At 50 feet in diameter, it carries 68 jumping horses and

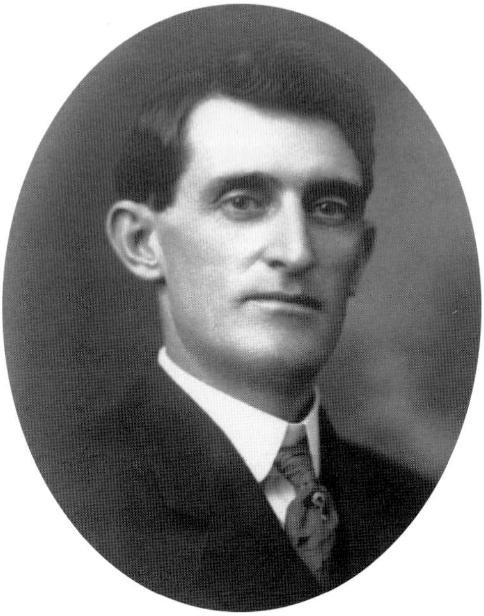

Austin McFadden:
His imagination first brought
the carousel to the
Minnesota State Fair.
Photo from the collection of his grandson, Paul Courtemanche

two chariots. For 75 years it ran only a few days each year at the state fair, so much of its original paint is intact — a rarity among antique carousels. The horses are the work of an exceptionally talented carver whose identity, until recently, was a mystery; we are using this book and the carousel's 100th birthday to give him the acclaim he deserves. But it was a carnival and amusement entrepreneur named Austin McFadden whose vision brought the carousel to Minnesota, and that's where our story begins.

The Minnesota State Fair was founded in the late 1800s to promote the state's agricultural activities. Organizers hoped to draw farmers from across the state to display their best crops and livestock, learn about the latest in farming techniques, and see modern equipment that could increase their productivity.

A series of regional fairs struggled for attendance before a permanent site became available in 1885 in the town of Hamline, now Falcon Heights, half-way between Saint Paul and Minneapolis. Almost from the beginning, entertainment added to the fair's appeal. Classic traveling carnival acts — the strong man, the fat lady, the fortune teller — amused gawkers and wowed the gullible.

Games of skill and chance were added, along with amusement rides. With this combination of serious-minded agricultural exhibits and slightly exotic entertainment the Minnesota State Fair become the largest in the country; by 1910 attendance was nearly double that of the next largest fair.

Minnesotans had disagreed over the years about how much entertainment should be offered. Some complained that certain sideshow attractions were scandalous, especially those featuring gambling or women in provocative dress. Periodically the Agricultural Society, which managed the fair, renewed its promise to keep things wholesome, and they changed vendors often in an effort to find the best quality, the most honest, the least offensive. But in September 1913 the women's division of the state labor bureau filed a complaint against "objectionable" sideshows. The Agricultural Society seemed to react strongly; in March 1914 a *St. Paul Daily News* headline claimed that the midway, where these colorful attractions operated, would close forever. The newspaper said the fair board would "depart from time-honored custom and put on an educational carnival, moral in nature." There would be no more concessionaires; the fair's managers would run everything.

Had they taken such drastic action, Minnesota's carousel would not have been built. But privately board members were concerned that without these attractions, gate receipts would fall by at least 20 percent, maybe more. In the midst of this discussion, Austin McFadden — himself a concession operator — had a bigger idea. McFadden, who lived in Grand Rapids, Michigan, had begun his career as a traveling showman, at one point teaching ballroom dance. He regularly crisscrossed the country visiting fairs, carnivals, and amusement parks in connection with his business, which eventually ranged from roller coasters to dance pavilions and from Baltimore to Venice Beach.

In fall 1913 McFadden asked the Agricultural Society for permission to establish two permanent rides on the fair grounds: a giant roller coaster and a very large merry-go-round. McFadden would own the machines and would operate and maintain them on a long-term contract. With these rides in permanent residence, he suggested, the fair could guarantee wholesome, crowd-pleasing entertainment. McFadden had to wait until spring 1914 for official approval of his contract. The fair's managers gave him favorable rates — 15 percent of his revenue each of the first three years and 25 percent the next seven years. They agreed to install his rides in a central location, not grouped with other amusements (which, despite their initial statements, they did not eliminate). With the deal finally completed in April, McFadden could order a roller coaster and a carousel, both of which had to be built, shipped to Minnesota, assembled, and made ready to operate by Labor Day, the fair's opening day.

The Minnesota State Fair was an unlikely home for a large, four-row carousel like the one McFadden bought. Most carousels of its size were installed at amusement parks, where they could operate for a long season to cover the investment in the machine. On the other hand, to be profitable at fairs and carnivals, which operated only a few days each year, a carousel needed to travel the circuit. It needed to come apart in sections to be quickly dismantled by a couple of workers, trucked to a new destination, and set up again. Horses on these carousels were small and lean, making them easier to carry. They were usually the same size and shape, making them interchangeable — no need to pause to figure out where each one should go.

McFadden's unusual challenge was to provide a permanent ride for a fair that ran only six days (not until the 1970s did it reach the current 12 days). To turn a profit, he had to earn as much revenue as possible in a few days *and* minimize his costs. McFadden turned to Philadelphia Toboggan Company, which was building massive, smooth-running machines; we think of PTC as the Cadillac of the industry. McFadden ordered a large carousel — 68 horses in four concentric rows, and two chariots — to accommodate lots of riders. With an even number of rows, all the horses would go up and down. To make them even more appealing, he made sure that the horses, especially those on the outer row, would be the finest that the company could turn out.

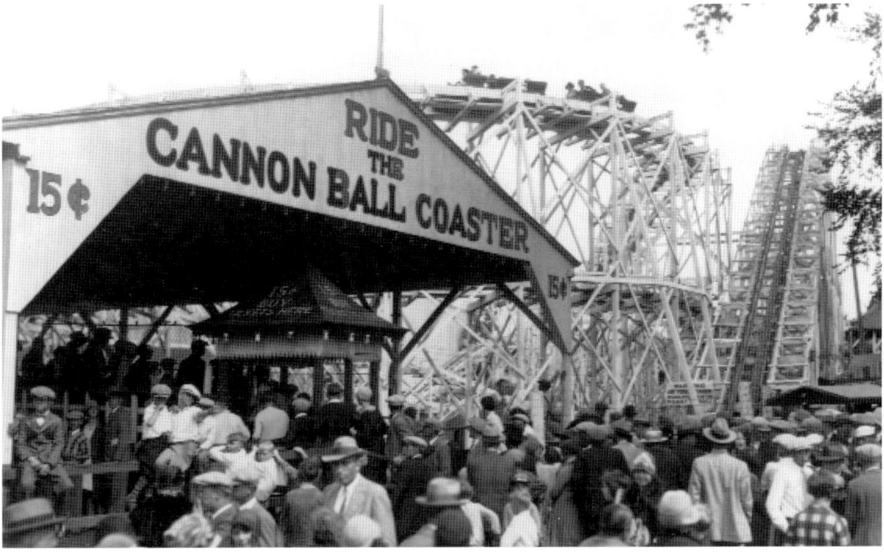

When Austin McFadden's new attractions were announced in 1914, the roller coaster got top billing. In 1928, when this photo was taken, it did big business. But it lasted only until 1935. The carousel turns 100 in 2014.
Photo used by permission of Minnesota State Fair

To focus his dollars on the horses, McFadden kept the body of the carousel quite plain. Most machines built for permanent installation were given elaborate sculptural trimmings on the rounding boards that define the upper structure, and on the housing that surrounds the motor. McFadden sacrificed those elements. There would be painted flourishes instead of carved ones, straight edges instead of curves, simplicity instead of excess. In 1915 the company would build an ornate three-row carousel with 44 horses for Seneca Park in Rochester, New York, for $9,000. By scaling back the decorations, McFadden was able to purchase a four-row carousel with 68 outstanding horses for only $8,500.

McFadden and PTC worked out another variation. The carousel and its outer-row horses are too large to be considered portable. Yet its parts are connected with easily removable fittings like those on portable carousels. Rounding board sections are held together with a pin that slides in and out with the tap of a hammer, rather than with more permanent bolts. Eighteen decorative shields, each with mirror and lights, are not bolted into place; they simply plug into electrical wiring and hang over the join between sections. Each of the 18 segments of carousel floor can be lifted out as a unit after undoing three bolts. And each horse can be lifted from its hanger by disengaging a pin, rather than undoing a bolt. These choices say that Austin McFadden was keeping his options open. If for any reason the carousel wasn't popular and profitable at the Minnesota State Fair, McFadden could move it elsewhere with relative ease.

On May 15, 1914, Austin McFadden signed a purchase agreement with PTC and paid the first installment of $1,000. He would pay another $4,000 when the machine was loaded onto a train to be shipped from Germantown, Pennsylvania, to Minnesota, and the final $3,500 within two weeks after it was completely assembled. His purchase would be the 33rd carousel created by the Philadelphia Toboggan Company, and in carousel circles it is still referred to as PTC33. The company was working on several other carousels, but most would be delivered in spring before parks opened for the season. This one had until mid-August to reach Minnesota. It was a tight schedule, but not impossible.

Typically, a carousel in a permanent location would be housed in a round pavilion topped by a clerestory — a set of windows circling the peak of the roof to allow light into the center of the building. McFadden built a windowless rectangular wooden building with seven solid garage doors across the front. A raised section of roof accommodated the height of the center pole but it had no windows. There was plenty of room for a band organ at the east end of the building, and McFadden installed a large and undoubtedly very loud one (it was later destroyed leaving no record of its make or model). With the doors open and the band organ playing, passersby would be drawn to the carousel no matter what the building looked like. And there would be passersby, because the building enjoyed a prominent location on busy Commonwealth Avenue, three short blocks inside the main gate.

PTC construction foreman Charles Bowditch traveled to Minnesota to supervise setup. He spent two weeks in town, managing assembly of hundreds of individual pieces: a carefully chosen center pole, 18 floor sections, dozens of precisely measured pieces of wooden frame, heavy iron gears, a drive mechanism, dozens of brass poles, electrical wiring, lights, horses, chariots. A properly made carousel is a triumph of compact, efficient engineering, but it must be carefully aligned, balanced, and lubricated. Once the horses were aboard and the adjustments made, workers would clean up the grease and wipe fingerprints off the brand-new brass poles. The carousel was ready. Or was it?

The 1914 fair opened Monday morning, September 7. There were no headlines about the new carousel, but people found their way to it as McFadden knew they would, and they lined up to buy their five-cent tickets. The ride was pleasantly full but not overcrowded; the first three rides carried 135 riders. Then suddenly, not two hours into its first day, the carousel shut down. It did not spin again until late Wednesday. State fair records say the "main bearing shaft" broke. That term isn't familiar in the carousel world, but we have come to believe it refers to the center pole — the 25-foot pine log which is crowned by a top bearing. Everything that rotates, including horses, chariots, floor sections, and rounding boards, is suspended from the center pole. It certainly seems to meet the description "main bearing shaft." On the other hand, center poles are sturdy; it's hard to imagine one failing. Besides, even working around the clock, how could they locate a suitable replacement (usually a perfectly straight long-leaf pitch pine not found in the Midwest), disassemble the carousel, and build it again, in less than three days?

The carousel has a feature that we have puzzled over for years. It seems out of character, but it might be explained by that first-day shut-down. The Philadelphia Toboggan Company is known for precise work — everything carefully measured, aligned, joined — and yet our carousel's center pole does not fit properly. It's a little banana-shaped; we always wondered how it passed inspection at PTC. Further, the pole is too narrow for the metal gear that must be attached near the middle, so shims have to be used, making it extremely difficult to mesh perfectly with the rest of the gears.

Even more surprisingly, the base has to be shimmed to fit snugly into the supporting structure — which would have been built in place specifically for this center pole. Why would PTC have relied on shims instead of building the structure to fit properly? Why would they have used a crooked pole? And why, when other PTC carousels have their number stamped into the pole at eye height in three-inch numerals, does our center pole have no number? In spite of our initial doubts and lingering astonishment, we have come to believe that there was indeed a problem with the original center pole and that a new one was quickly substituted. It is not ideal, and its irregularity complicated the process of adjusting the gears when we moved the carousel. But it has already lasted 100 years and it shows no sign of failing.

The carousel drew just over 17,000 riders in its not-quite-four days of operation in 1914, and 27,000 in six days the following year. Austin McFadden operated both the carousel and the roller coaster until his contract ran out in 1924. He had continued to expand his activities, especially in Southern California. In 1922 he and two other investors built a new ocean-front pier in Venice with an immense ballroom, a roller coaster, and several new thrill rides. The entire pier burned down in 1924, destroying all of the property and concessions. Dropping his Minnesota connections and perhaps others across the country, McFadden turned his attention to rebuilding the pier. He built a home in Malibu, invested in other lucrative business opportunities, and died a wealthy man.

With McFadden's departure, a Minneapolis man named Lew Hoffman became the manager and public face of the carousel for the next 20 years. An Austrian immigrant whose original last name was Niederhofer, he was sometimes listed in state fair records as the carousel's owner and other times as the agent of an unnamed owner. On rare occasions in those years, the name Martin Schuemaker appeared as owner. Whatever their arrangement, by 1944 both men had died and the new owner was Hoffman's sister, Lena Niederhofer Hesik.

In 1939, Hoffman and the carousel had an especially difficult summer. On June 2, a house trailer parked in front of the building

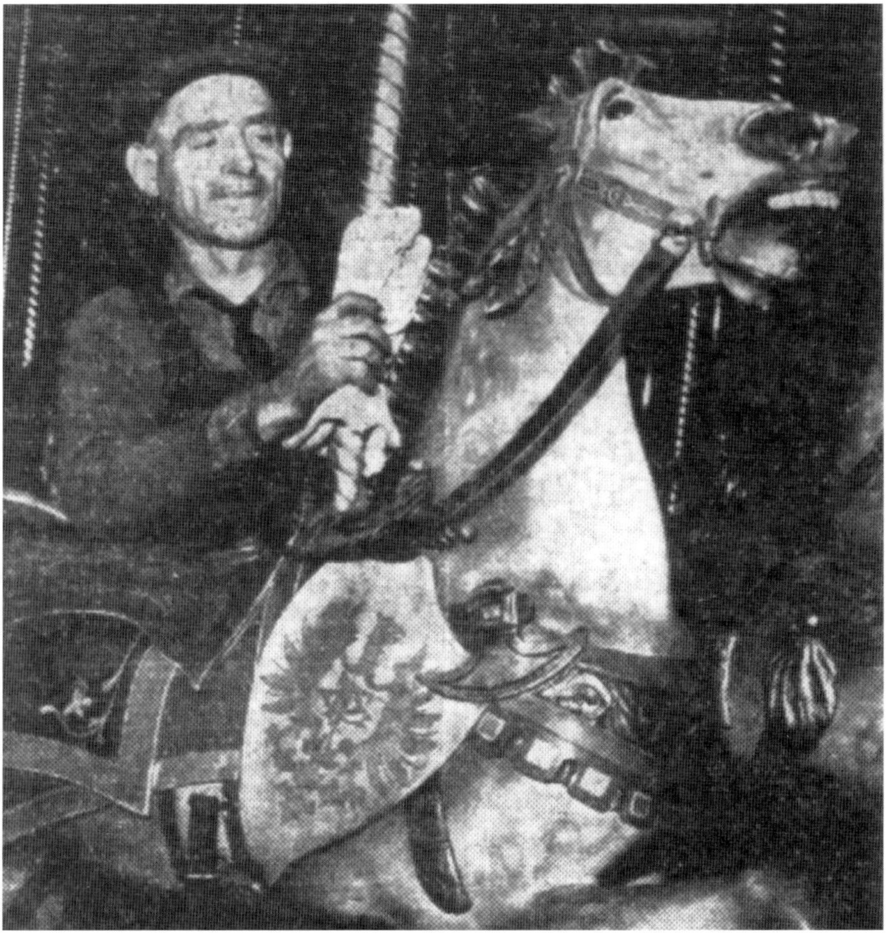

There are only three known photos of the carousel taken before the 1939 fire. This one, from the August 30, 1935, *Minneapolis Tribune*, shows Lou Hitzmann polishing brass—a daily activity that still happens today.
Photo courtesy of the Minnesota Historical Society

caught fire. When firefighters arrived, flames had spread to the wooden carousel building and climbed to the roof. A firefighter once told us that had someone opened a door to the building before the men were right there with hoses trained on the flames, the rush of oxygen into the building would have instantly sent the fire out of control. The carousel would have been a total loss.

As it was, six of the carousel's 18 sections suffered some damage. The two outside-row horses nearest the burning trailer lost all

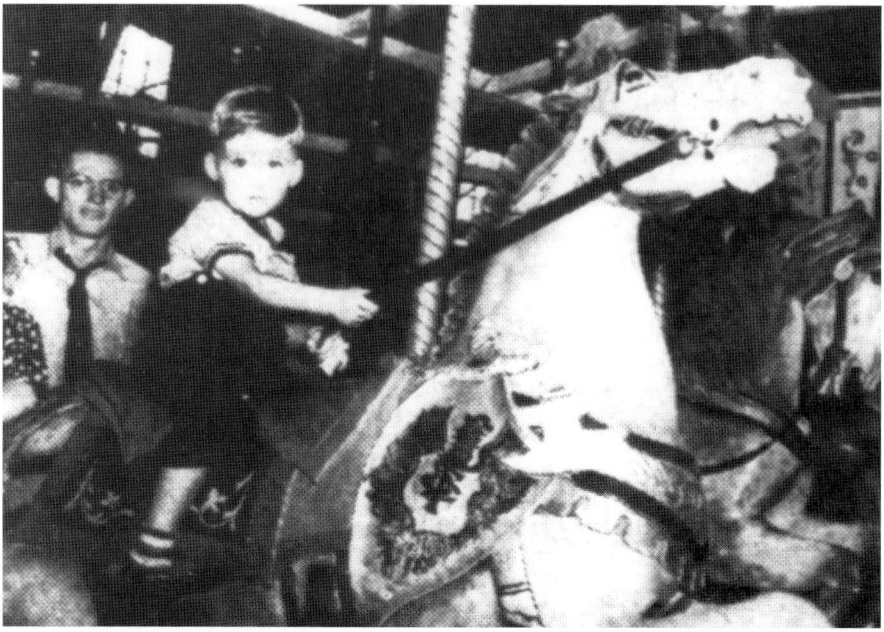

Two-and-a-half-year-old Donald Krois has his first ride on the carousel in this photo from the *Saint Paul Dispatch,* August 29, 1939. In 1989 his mother sent us the clipping, reinforcing for us the generational appeal of the carousel. *Photo courtesy of the Minnesota Historical Society*

the paint on their right sides and their surfaces were turned to checkered charcoal. Radiating out from those two, the horses in front and behind them and the second-row horses next to them were damaged but less severely. Overhead, two of the 18 fiber-board rounding board paintings were destroyed by fire and most of the rest water-damaged. Mounted atop the rounding boards were wooden crowns, each with a carved lion's head; again those nearest the fire were destroyed and others damaged. Burning bits of the building's roof fell to the carousel platform and smoldered, leaving indentations that can still be seen. We know from the PTC ledger that there were painted ceiling panels atop the carousel's 18 sections, but we cannot say with certainty what they looked like. Clearly, they were damaged by the fire and discarded. The carousel's band organ, standing in the corner where the fire originated, was reduced to ashes. But firefighters had saved the carousel itself — something of a miracle considering how many wooden carousels have been lost in flames even as recently as 2013.

Hoffman had the fire-damaged horses painted over wherever they needed it. He had two new rounding boards and crowns made, and he had two lion's faces painted on the flat surface to replace the lost carvings. He replaced all the original fiberboard rounding board paintings with tin panels and hired sign painters to create new drawings meant to portray the pastoral scenes depicted in the originals. The effect was not great art, but the drawings created a record of the original themes that would be invaluable many years later when we restored the machine. With the building cleaned up and recorded music substituted for the band organ, the carousel operated for the 1939 fair.

But Hoffman's busy year wasn't over. For 25 years the carousel had stood at the intersection of Commonwealth Avenue, which ran east-and-west, and Underwood Street, which ran from the carousel building to the fair's southern edge. Now Underwood was to be extended to the north, and the carousel was in the way. Hoffman carefully dismantled the carousel and its building and reassembled them 100 feet to the east, where they would remain for another 50 years.

Lew Hoffman's sister, Lena Hesik, took over the carousel at a difficult time. She ran it for the 1944 fair, but there were no fairs in 1945 and 1946. The 1945 fair was cancelled as part of the war effort; the country's trains were needed to transport troops and supplies. The next year, the country was experiencing a polio epidemic. The 1947 fair was well attended, and the carousel shared in that success, but it is perhaps not surprising that Mrs. Hesik began to look for a buyer. Happily, she found one, just across the street.

As a young man, William "Bill" Brede began to develop his father's small sign company into a large enterprise supplying "pipe and drape" display materials and other trade show necessities. The sign company did many jobs on the fairgrounds, and the personable Brede built on his connections to develop a profitable set of holdings. Austin McFadden had introduced new concessions

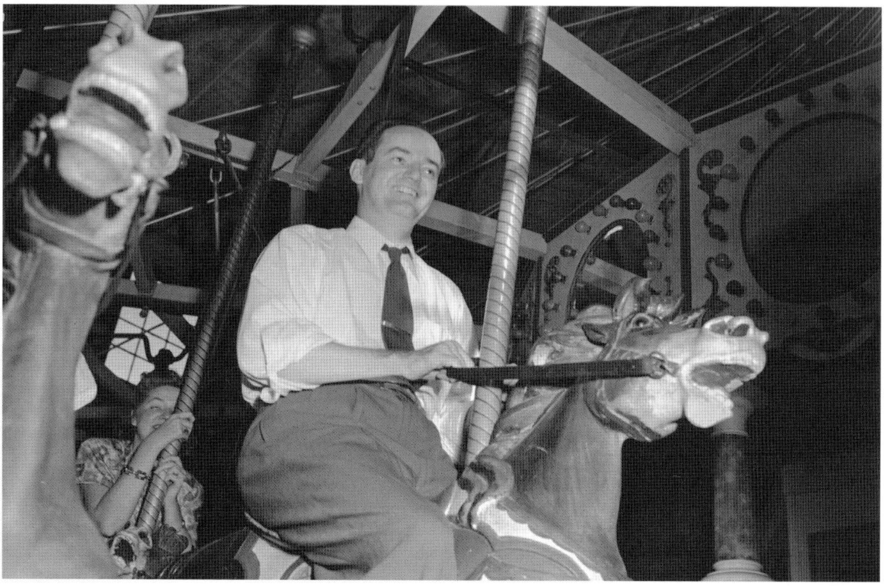

The carousel was a popular meeting place for folks at the fair, and a photo opportunity for statewide office-seekers. Minneapolis mayor Hubert Humphrey, taking a spin in 1947, was preparing a 1948 run for U.S. Senate. *Photo courtesy of the Minnesota Historical Society*

across the country; Bill Brede introduced new attractions to his home state. He brought the Pronto Pup to Minnesota in 1947, quickly making it the quintessential fair-food-on-a-stick. He had initiated the popular beer garden back in 1933 and it was just across the street from the carousel, where his daughters Shirley and Mary liked to be when they weren't busy working. Mary was partial to a horse with an unadorned animal-skin saddle; Shirley liked several of the brighter ones and thought Mary felt sorry for the plainest one. They both loved the carousel, and so did their dad, and in 1949 he bought it.

By this time, years of aging varnish were turning the horses and their colorful trappings a deep brown. Brede decided to brighten things up. He employed some of his sign painters to paint over the scenes on the rounding boards with a bright red-on-white scroll design. (It may well have been Brede painters who created those scenes after the 1939 fire.) They painted the horses' mouths bright red and added black swashes near the eyes to make them look fierce. Using mostly red, green, and black, they touched up carved bridles and saddle blankets. They repainted scratched saddles in brown and horse shoes in silver. In the 1990s when our volunteers were restoring the horses' original paint, we had to remove these swatches of color as well as the darkened varnish. But we understood exactly why Bill Brede had them painted. Like Austin McFadden and Lew Hoffman before him, he wanted to attract riders.

Over the years both daughters and their families pitched in at various Brede-owned fair enterprises. Shirley Brede Reibold and Mary Brede Blinstrup each managed the carousel for a time, and when the Reibold and Blinstrup children were old enough they sold tickets or worked on the carousel. In 1983, four years after Bill Brede's death, his daughters divided the concessions. Mary pleaded for the carousel, and she got it. A short time later, she and her family began looking to sell. Their final year of ownership would be 1988, the carousel's 74th year of operation at the fair and the 39th year as a Brede family enterprise. By then, the carousel had become more than just an amusement ride.

2

The Unknown Carver

Austin McFadden, the Michigan man who dreamed up a permanent carousel for the Minnesota State Fair, had the good fortune to call on Philadelphia Toboggan Company at a time when an especially talented craftsman headed up the carving shop.

This is no small thing. The master carver set the tone for the entire shop's work, and his distinctive style in creating the figures — be they horses or the variety of animals known as menagerie figures — gave each carousel its unique personality. To a carousel connoisseur today, a figure by a heralded master carver like Gustav Dentzel, Daniel Muller, Charles Carmel, or Frank Carretta can be especially valued — worth travelling to see on a carousel, or, for some, worth collecting. Perhaps this is why in 1988, when 20 of our carousel's horses were listed for sale in an auction catalog, they were described as the work of Frank Carretta, a noted and award-winning carver for PTC. But the catalog was wrong.

The carver who brought Minnesota's carousel to life was a Scottish American named David Lightfoot. A modest man, Lightfoot left little evidence of his role for carousel historians to discover.

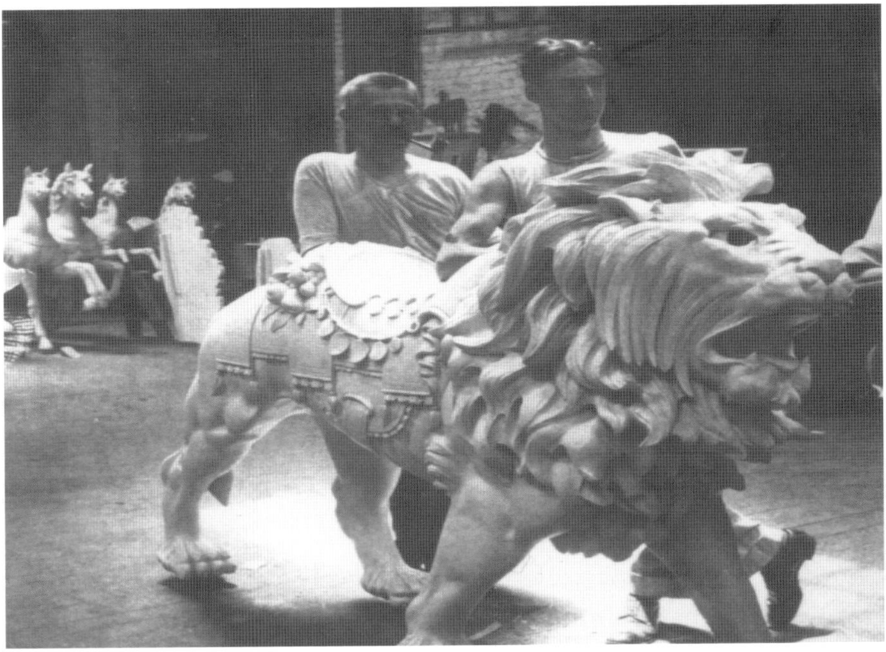

This photo was taken at the E. Joy Morris factory in 1903—around the time PTC bought all of their stock. The young man at right is David Lightfoot, who worked on carving this lion. Another photo Lightfoot saved from this day showed Frank Carretta carving a similar lion's head.
From the collection of David Lightfoot's daughter, Marjorie Maben-Briel

Fred Fried, whose 1964 book *A Pictorial History of the Carousel* was the first comprehensive history of carousels, filled the void by saying Frank Carretta must have been supplying PTC's figures in 1914. Fried's book was used widely as a resource, and others shared his assumption as a statement of fact. But in 1988 Fried himself told us he'd been wrong, and after our carousel made headlines around the world, the families of both David Lightfoot and Austin McFadden reached out to us with photos, artifacts, and recollections, enabling us to piece together the real story. We are happy to provide an important chapter to what is known about Minnesota's carousel and, in the process, to give David Lightfoot his proper place in history.

Before Fred Fried's book, many people had assumed that America's oldest hand-carved wooden carousels were imported from

Europe. But Fried told of a handful of European immigrants who were skilled woodcarvers, had some knowledge of Europe's carousels, and developed their own machines in this country in the 1850s and 1860s. Like carousels in Europe, the first American machines were powered by people or horses; then came steam and, finally, electricity. As each of these pioneers developed a machine that could be produced at a profit, he started a company and hired other woodcarvers, also immigrants. Typically, these carvers had begun their careers in Europe creating elaborate church altars and elegant furnishings. Finding little demand for their skills in America, they went to work for carousel companies that grew up primarily in Philadelphia, New York, and Kansas.

Carousel figures produced in Philadelphia were distinctively realistic, with well-proportioned bodies and natural expressions; the approach is now called Philadelphia Style. Trappings were based on reality but interpreted with a bit of flair to give a sense of motion and speed. They might be decorated with small animals for example, or with patriotic themes or military gear. Even within the traditions of the Philadelphia Style, a strong master carver endowed figures with his own recognizable style.

Carousels built in New York were flashier, designed to operate at Coney Island and other highly competitive amusement parks. Coney Island Style carvers were less interested in anatomical accuracy, instead creating fanciful and ornate features like wildly flowing manes, jeweled trappings, and exaggerated expressions. A third style, County Fair, refers to smaller portable machines, built mainly in upstate New York and Abilene and Topeka, Kansas. They bore vivid but small and light-weight figures designed to be easily moved to the next location on the circuit. Wild West symbols were popular themes.

Philadelphia already had a couple of carousel factories, including the highly successful one founded by Gustav Dentzel, when businessman Henry Auchy founded the Philadelphia Toboggan Company in 1904. Auchy's factory would manufacture carousels and roller coaster cars, known as toboggans. He was experienced with machinery, not carving. To get production underway, he bought out the nearby E. Joy Morris Company and its enormous stock of menagerie figures, and he hired several experienced carvers on a freelance basis. As a result, PTC was able to build and deliver five three-row carousels carrying 220 figures in just its first seven months of operation. They produced eight more over the next two years. Most were three-row carousels with menagerie figures including giraffes, rabbits, lions, deer, cats, and dogs, still from the E. Joy Morris stock. But the company was beginning to introduce four- and five-row carousels, and with the hiring of Leo B. Zoller as its first master carver in 1907, PTC produced no more menagerie figures.

Zoller and crew created large horses that were not especially well proportioned. In fact, by 1910 and 1911, with even the supply of E. Joy Morris horses used up, PTC's horses had become especially awkward, with elongated faces, strangely high-set eyes, and knobby, distorted joints. Could that be the reason the company sold only two carousels in those years?

By 1912, Zoller was gone, PTC horses had become well proportioned, the company was building ever-more-lavish carousels on which to place them, and orders flowed in. Who led the turnaround, which includes the period in which our carousel was made? The company kept a hand-written ledger which shows payments to carvers, but from 1910 to 1916 it never identifies a head carver. To put this "mystery of the unknown carver" into context, let us mention two others.

John Zalar was PTC's head carver from 1916 to 1922. He had worked with Charles Looff, celebrated for developing the more flamboyant Coney Island Style. Zalar's work remained essentially faithful to the Philadelphia Style, but sometimes there would be a tell-tale flash of Coney Island — a wild-eyed look here, an exaggerated drooping tongue there.

Frank Carretta, PTC's last and most celebrated head carver, earned national carver-of-the-year awards for his dramatic and elegant horses in the mid-1920s. The company took him to annual conventions of the National Association of Amusement Parks, where he demonstrated his techniques as part of the PTC exhibit.

A reporter from the *Philadelphia Bulletin* wrote that at the 1927 convention in Chicago, more people were drawn to watch Carretta work than to admire the large assortment of new equipment. The admiring reporter described Carretta working on a big block of basswood with his array of specialized chisels — narrow, curved, hooked, flat — and the mallet with which he carefully tapped them. "How many horses has he made?" wrote the reporter. "One every week for many years. And every one is different."

Fred Fried posited that Frank Carretta must have been with PTC in the years between Zoller and Zalar. Nobody else was known to be capable of such fine work, he reasoned, so who else could it have been? Besides, Carretta lived right in the neighborhood. Even if he didn't hold the title of head carver, he must have been a loyal company man, content to do the work and stay out of the limelight.

The fact is that *somebody* was content to do the work and stay out of the limelight, but it wasn't Frank Carretta.

In 1988, the catalog for the auction that included 20 horses from our carousel carried an essay by carousel expert Marge Swenson describing the horses as Carretta's work. On the day of the auction, when we were still frantically negotiating to purchase the carousel before its first horse came up for sale, Fred Fried spoke to us for a moment. He said something we didn't fully understand at the time, and we couldn't pursue it just then. "Marge Swenson should have known better," he said, his eyes flashing. "This isn't Carretta's work. It's Lightfoot's."

Shortly after we acquired the carousel, Fried invited Peter to his New York home to review his accumulation of documents relating to Philadelphia Toboggan Company. Among them was an interview Fried had taped with Frank Carretta. The carver told Fried he had worked a few months for PTC in 1903 — seemingly just when PTC was acquiring the E. Joy Morris company. After that, Carretta moved to Gustav Dentzel's factory for six years, "until the old man died" in 1909 and his sons took over the company. Carretta said he then spent 16 years carving Victrola cabinets for Victor Talking Machine Company. On the tape, Fried was clearly surprised to

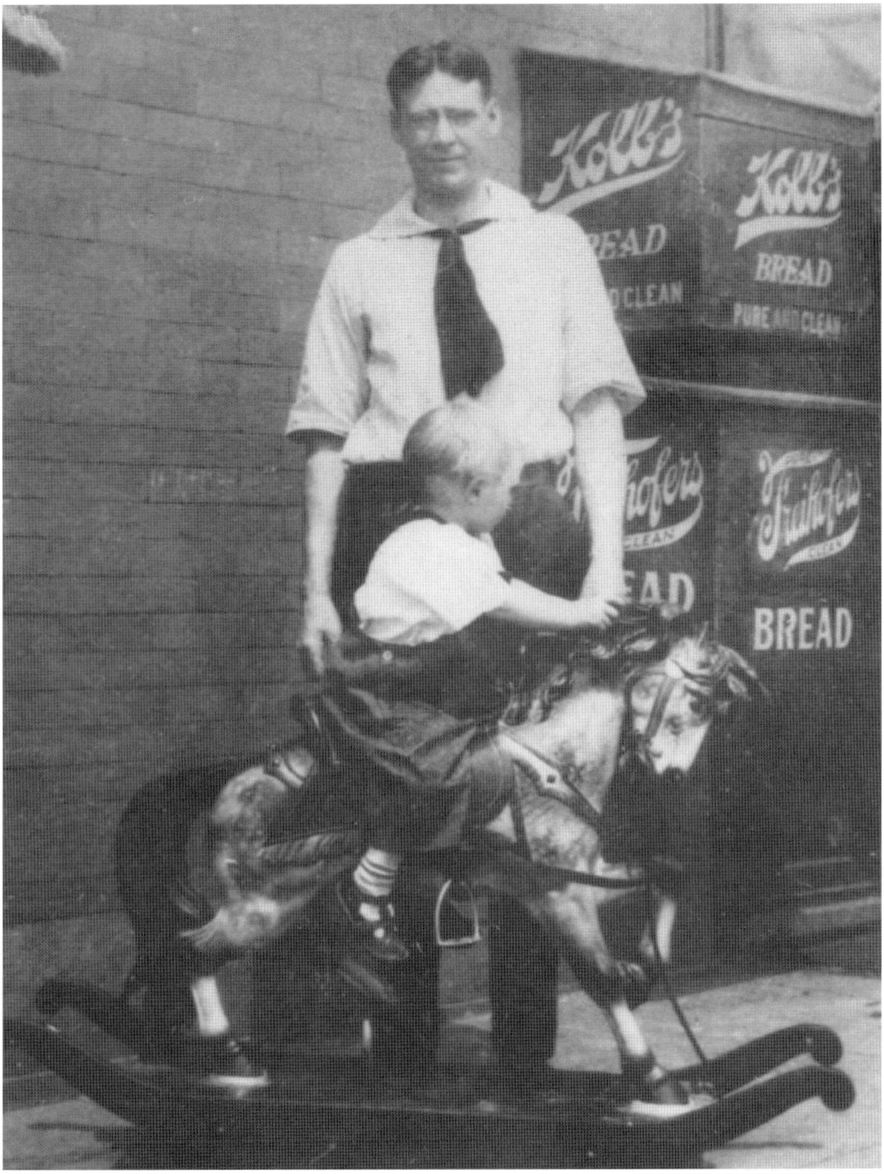

David Lightfoot with son, Malcolm, riding on Smokey. Malcolm was born in 1913. David carved Smokey during 1914, the same year he was creating Minnesota's carousel. *From the collection of Marjorie Maben-Briel*

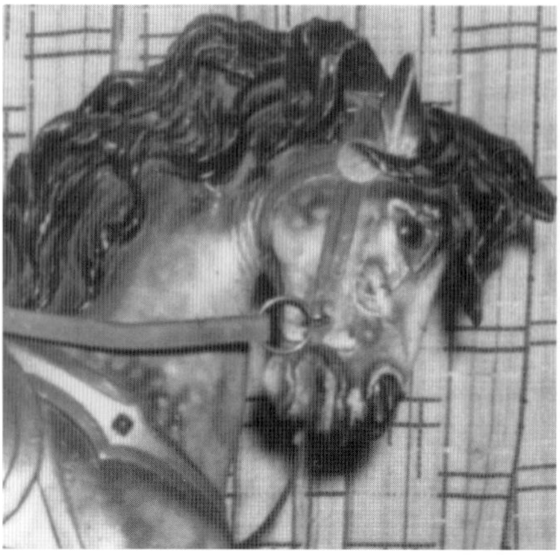

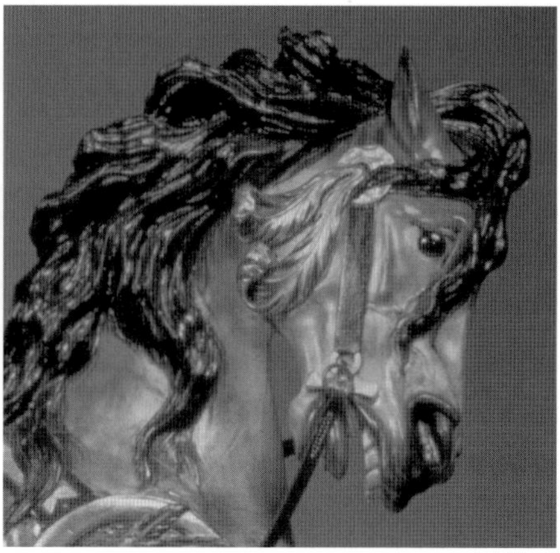

The head on the left is Smokey. The one on the right is from an outside row horse on PTC33. We are convinced they were both carved by David Lightfoot.

Photo on left from the collection of Marjorie Maben-Briel. Photo on right is by Steve McHugh

hear this. After all, his own book said Carretta joined PTC in 1912. In the interview he made sure he heard it right: Carretta didn't return to PTC until about 1925.

Somehow between the time Fred Fried learned he'd been wrong about Carretta and the time we encountered him at the auction in 1988, he had become convinced that our carousel was Lightfoot's work. But despite all his contacts and research, Fried had been unable to find conclusive evidence. The PTC ledger showed payments to David Lightfoot as an employee, but it didn't specify a head carver. At the time Peter visited Fried's home, we still had a half-million dollars to raise and a carousel to move to a new location. We promised ourselves we would return to finding David Lightfoot when things settled down. Instead, you might say he found us.

One day in late 1989 — before things had settled down at all — we received a letter from Marjorie Maben-Briel of Tucson, Arizona. A story about the carousel from the *Christian Science Monitor* had been picked up in a San Francisco paper. Remembering that Mrs. Maben-Briel's father had worked for PTC, her daughter-in-law sent her the story. Mrs. Maben-Briel's letter said her father had worked for PTC about the time our carousel was made, and she had some pictures. Would we like to see them? Peter wrote back saying we'd love copies of the pictures, and asking questions including this one: "Did you ever hear the name David Lightfoot?" Back came the reply: "David Lightfoot was my father."

Of the photos she sent, one instantly grabbed our attention. It showed her father and year-old brother Malcolm in 1914 with a wooden rocking horse her father had carved. The horse, which the family named Smokey, had a downturned head with a full, rounded mane, and it looked remarkably like three distinctive outer-row horses on our carousel. We could also see similarities between Smokey's saddle and trappings and those used on our carousel. But there was more. Over the whole course of his life, David Lightfoot had saved only 36 photos related to his years as a carousel carver. Three of those photos featured horses with trappings nearly identical to three of our most exceptional horses: the lead horse, the pinto pony, and the alligator horse. There could be no question: David Lightfoot was indeed the carver of PTC33.

Of his 36 carousel photos only three showed co-workers. One was a man who Mrs. Maben-Briel said her father had admired, and whose name she remembered as "Mr. Beretta." It was a photo of Frank Carretta carving a lion's head in the E. Joy Morris shop in about 1903—probably taken on the same day as the photo of young Lightfoot with his lion. And while we can't confirm that they remained friends, Mrs. Maben-Briel seemed to think they had.

In 1916 David Lightfoot went back to school to become an osteopath. This was a new specialty at the time, offered by only a few programs either as part of a medical degree or as a more limited holistic alternative. If he chose the latter, as seems to be the case, he received special training in the human musculoskeletal system and then specialized in stretching and massaging muscles and joints. It's easy to understand his attraction to the field; his interest in anatomical structure and musculature helped bring his carousel horses to life.

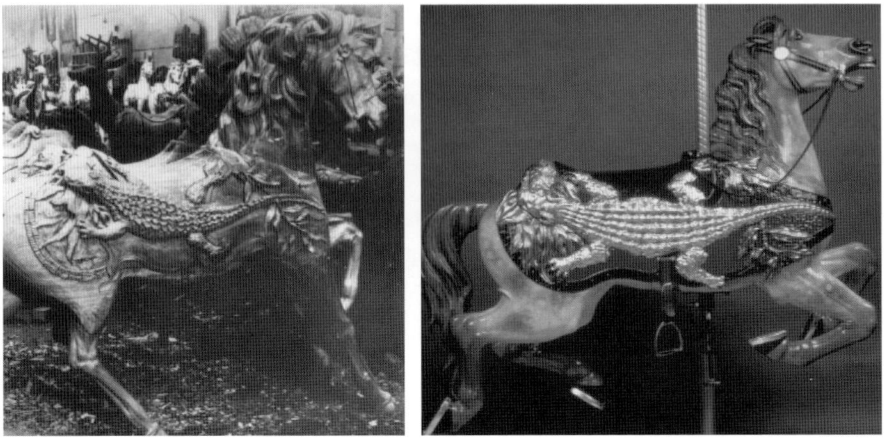

The photo on the left, from about 1903, is of a horse carved at the E. Joy Morris factory. The photo was among David Lightfoot's effects when he died. The horse on the right is on Cafesjian's Carousel and was carved by Lightfoot. The trappings on the two horses match in tiny details, including the way the edge of the saddle blanket is segmented.
Photo on left from the collection of Marjorie Maben-Briel. Photo on right is by Jerry Mathiason

Mrs. Maben-Briel told us that Smokey had been sold to an antique dealer in San Francisco in the 1960s. We promised ourselves that some day we would seek publicity on the West Coast to try to find him. That day has yet to come, but we have learned that Lightfoot created at least two more rocking horses nearly identical to Smokey. One went to Austin McFadden, who also had a young son at the time. We believe that McFadden saw the partially completed Smokey when he visited PTC in 1914, and that he asked Lightfoot to carve another. McFadden's family still had that horse when they contacted us a few years ago, and we were able to tell them more about the horse itself and about their grandfather's role in bringing our carousel into existence. As we write this, the McFadden family's horse is the centerpiece of a display at the carousel, on loan to Our Fair Carousel from the McFadden grandchildren.

Several years ago, a nearly identical rocking horse turned up on the cover of a Sotheby's auction catalog. We know only that it had been owned by a collector, that it was not sold in the auction, and that it had enough minor differences to show that it was not

Smokey. We would love to know more about those two rocking horses, but in any event they have confirmed for us that David Lightfoot was the head carver on our carousel and others that bear his stylistic imprint. Carousels in St. Louis, Georgia, and Australia, all carved between 1912 and 1916, carry horses that are certainly by Lightfoot. His work, long attributed to his friend, the illustrious Frank Carretta, deserves to be known and appreciated as the work of one David Lightfoot.

We should note that Lightfoot did not carve every horse aboard our carousel. In 1913 PTC had purchased six horses — three jumpers and three standers — from Charles Carmel, a highly respected carver and carousel builder in the Coney Island tradition. Carmel had invested heavily in an exceptional new carousel he planned to operate at Coney Island, only to see the entire amusement park burn down the day before it opened in 1911. Financially devastated, Carmel sold his remaining stock and went back to carving for other companies. Minnesotans are fortunate that three beautiful Carmel jumpers — a large one on the outside row and two smaller ones on inner rows — were placed on the carousel built for Austen McFadden. Finally, six very small and rather plain horses were pulled from stock to complete the inside row.

When the horses were finished, long-time PTC contractor Gus Weiss painted them, one as a pinto and the rest dapple-gray. Meanwhile, scenery painter Max Soltmann was creating 18 pastoral scenes on fiberboard for the carousel's rounding boards, as he did for all of PTC's carousels.

By 1914, PTC had built more than 30 carousels. The company had recovered from the poor carving and low sales of 1911 and 1912, and they wanted potential buyers to know it. Their advertising that year declared, "We make the best and finest carrousels at right prices. Come see us!" Austen McFadden took them up on that invitation, and he worked with them to design the perfect carousel for his needs: plain-spoken architecture, two handsome carved chariots, and 68 stunning jumping horses, most of them carved by David Lightfoot.

3

'Let's See What We Can Do'

Very few who visited the big carousel at the Minnesota State Fair in summer 1988 had any idea that even as they rode, plans were underway to take the carousel out of operation forever. The idea was unthinkable, really. The carousel had been on the fairgrounds since 1914 with no sign of leaving. We were among those who mistakenly assumed that the carousel was owned by the fair itself. We'd have been surprised to learn that it was privately owned and astonished that the family who owned it had been trying to sell it for years. In fact they had already sold it once.

In the early 1980s, after long-time owner Bill Brede's death, the ride passed to his daughter Mary Brede Blinstrup and her family, husband Bart and children Bill and Clare. They sold it to Bergerud & Whitney, a business partnership intending to operate it as part of a new development in downtown Minneapolis. But when the partners' plans fell through they defaulted on payments and the Blinstrups got the carousel back. Still hoping to find another buyer, they were reluctant to sign the customary contract guaranteeing that the carousel would operate at the fair in 1989. But the carousel occupied a prime location, and the fair board wanted to know the site would be occupied. There was already tension between the board and the family over another attraction, and the board pressed for a commitment. Instead, the Blinstrups consigned the carousel to Guernsey's auction house in New York.

Financially, their timing was exquisite. Antique carousels and their hand-crafted wooden figures were at the peak of popularity, admired as examples of American art and craft. Collectors were increasingly eager to buy them, and prices had risen accordingly. Now Arlan Ettinger, president of Guernsey's, estimated that sold individually, the 68 horses and two chariots would bring more than $1 million. Ridership at the fair had been growing steadily, but even with 80,000 riders as they had in 1988, it would take 20 years to bring in a million dollars.

To fetch the best prices, Ettinger and the Blinstrups decided not to sell all the horses at once. Instead, 20 horses and one chariot were pulled off the carousel and trucked to New York for a December 10 auction. The Blinstrups worked quietly, hoping to keep the information out of the media. For one thing, there were still 48 potentially high-value horses on the carousel in a not-very-secure building at the fairgrounds. For another, people would not be happy with this news.

As the horses traveled toward New York the auction was being publicized to antique dealers, especially those specializing in carousel figures. A few of these people had ties to Minnesota and recognized the carousel's value to the community, not just as a collection of figures but as a ride enjoyed by generations of families. We have heard a handful of stories about people who heard the news and set about contacting reporters and anyone else they could think of who might help prevent the breakup of the machine. One such person was Pat McGinnis, an antiques dealer in upstate New York who had lived in Minnesota and served as Burnsville's city manager. McGinnis learned about the auction directly from his friend Arlan Ettinger, who thought he might be interested in bidding on some of the Minnesota horses. Instead, he used his old contacts to leak the story. Thanks to McGinnis and other tipsters, by early November both daily papers were pursuing it.

The story broke Friday, November 11, in Minneapolis' *Star Tribune.* Reporter Mike Kaszuba wrote that 20 horses were to be sold on Saturday, December 10, and that efforts to save them "may be too late." Kaszuba reported that the state fair board had been offered a chance to buy the carousel but had decided the asking price was too high. James Sinclair, who headed up the fair's dealings with concessions, defended their decision: "Sure, there may be those who wish to see it remain," Sinclair said, "and it probably has sentimental value to some. Let's put it this way, this is a public institution. We're a creature of the legislature....I'm not sure that would be any kind of wise investment." Reporter Kaszuba noted that the carousel had been a significant part of the fair for 74 years. "Among the fair's hundreds of attractions, the carousel is rivaled in longevity only by such mainstays as the grandstand, built in 1910; Ye Old Mill, a canal boat ride that made its debut in 1915, and the John Deere exhibit, a fixture at the fair since 1905."

The *Star Tribune* story also placed the carousel in a national context. Nancy Loucks, editor of the monthly magazine *Carousel News & Trader,* told Kaszuba that the carousel was unique because its horses, having been ridden only a few days each year, still wore their original paint. Loucks said individual horses might sell for $20,000 to $30,000 or even more. "I don't know of another carousel around that compares with it," she said. She told Kaszuba she had been trying to find a buyer nationally since learning of the planned sale in late October. "It's a shame to break up a beautiful carousel like that." The story added that if a bid of at least $1.08 million were made on the carousel it would be sold intact, rather than horse by horse, to the highest bidder.

We — Peter and Nancy — learned about the story the next day. Our first response was just like that of so many other folks: "No! How can this be? Won't somebody stop this from happening?" And then Peter said something that would change our lives for the next 25 years:

"Let's see what we can do."

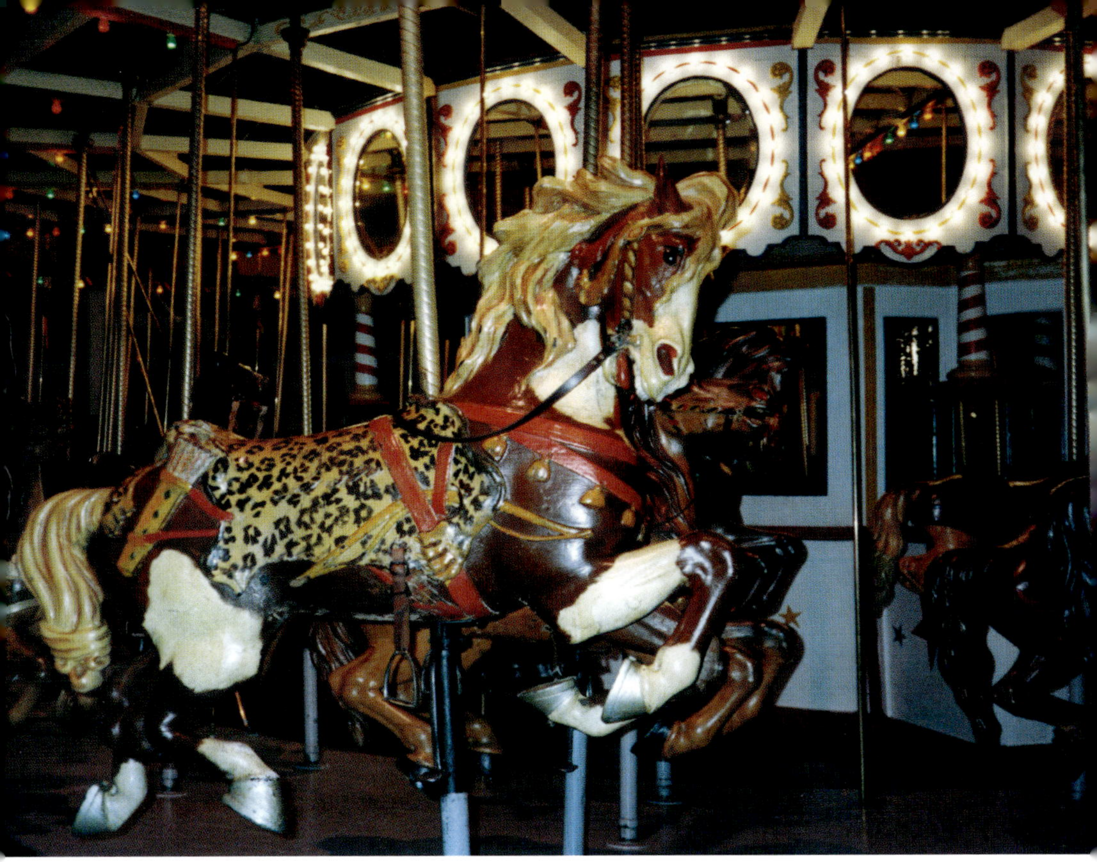

Realistically beautiful horses captured fairgoers' imaginations, and the pinto, fully repainted around 1949, was a favorite. Never the "world's largest merry-go-round," the carousel drew crowds day and night during the 1989 Minnesota State Fair as the nonprofit Our Fair Carousel fought to save it. *Upper photo by Barbara J. Hanson*

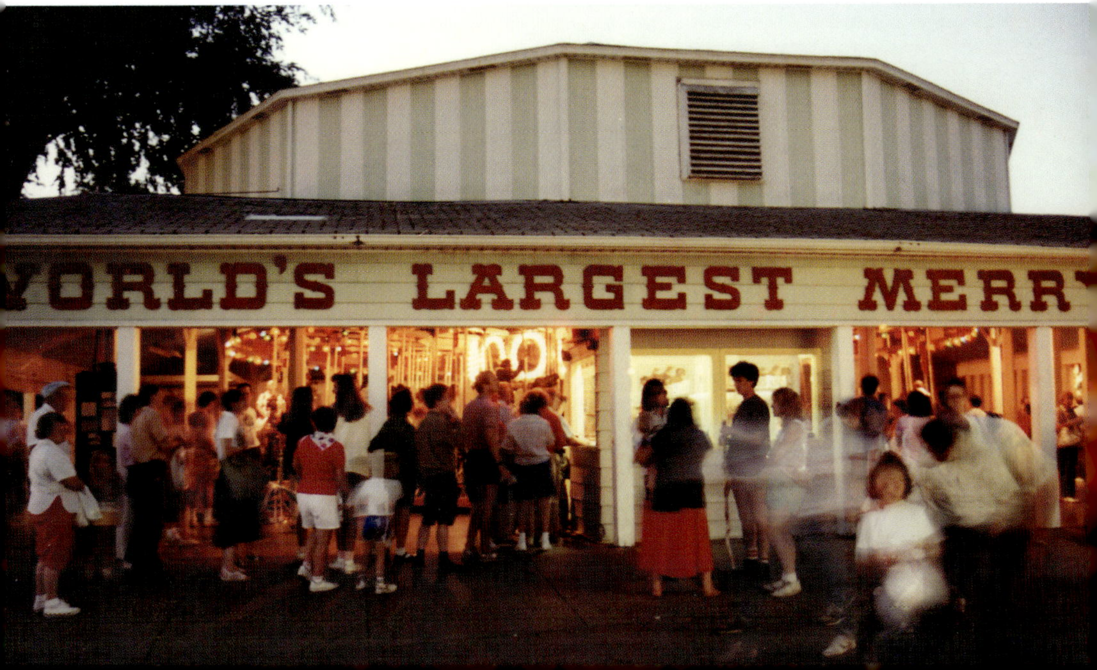

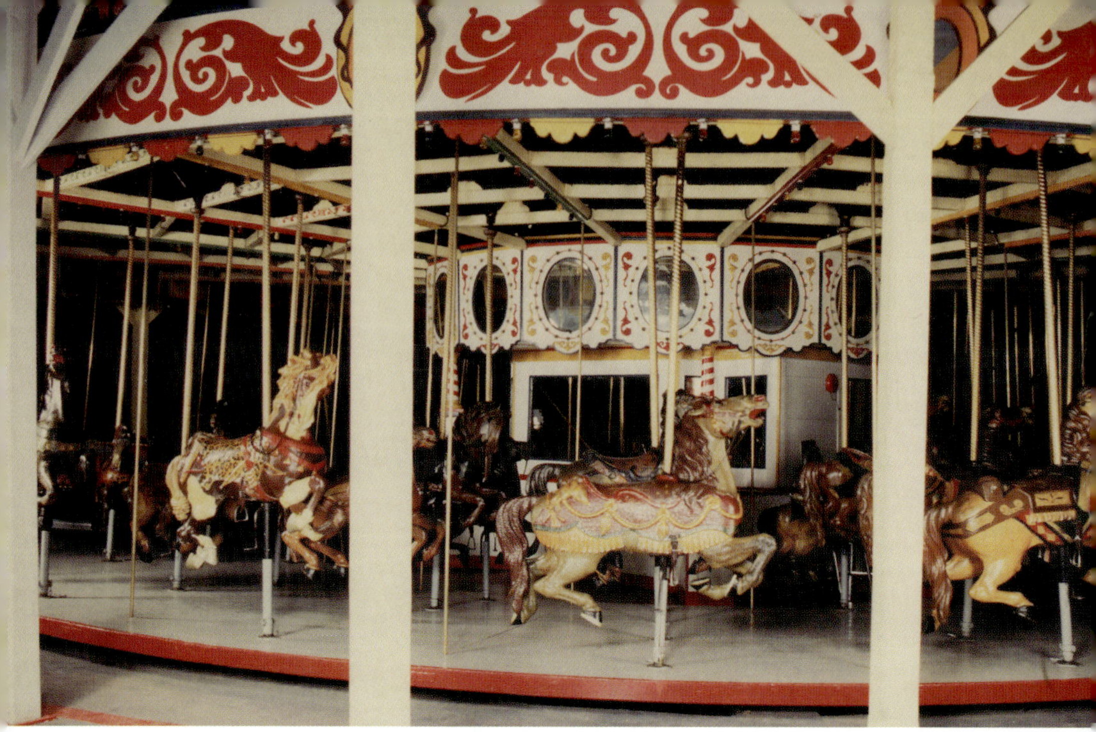

The carousel at the fairgrounds in 1988, top, and at Como Park in 1999, below, restored to look like it did in 1914. Scenery panels on the original rounding boards were destroyed by fire and water in 1939. Decorative parts, repainted in 1939 and again about 1950, were restored by Our Fair Carousel volunteers in 1990. *Photos by Steve McHugh, above, and Jerry Mathiason, below*

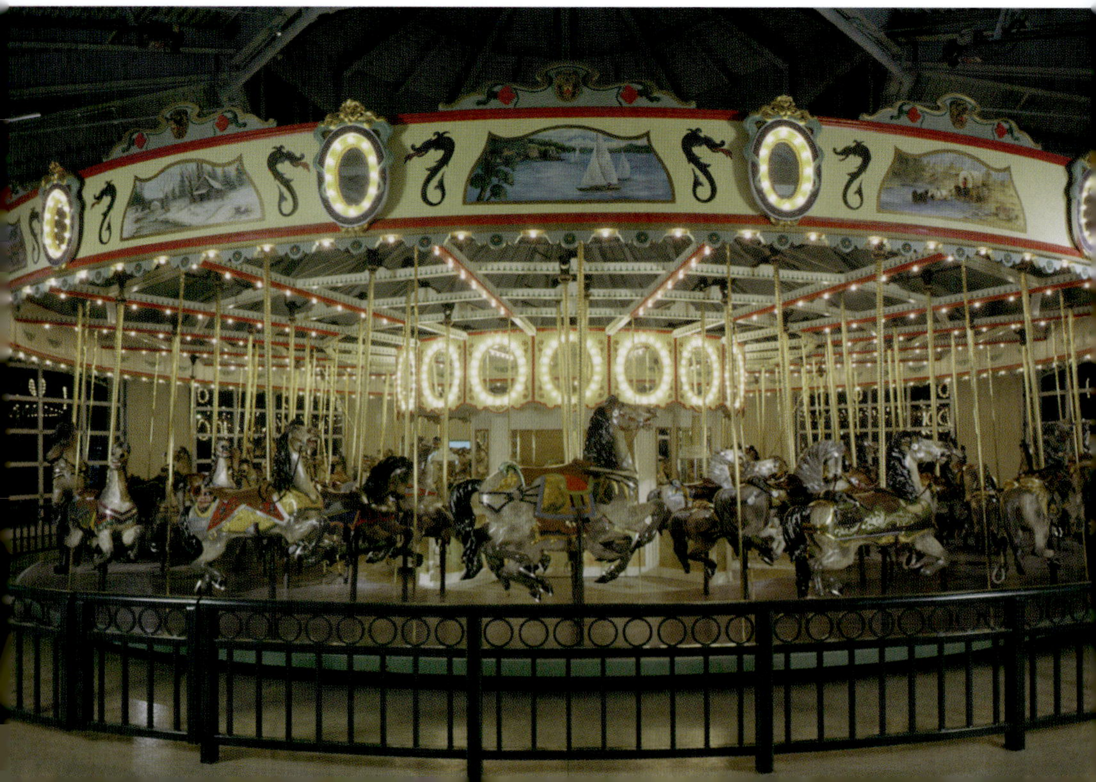

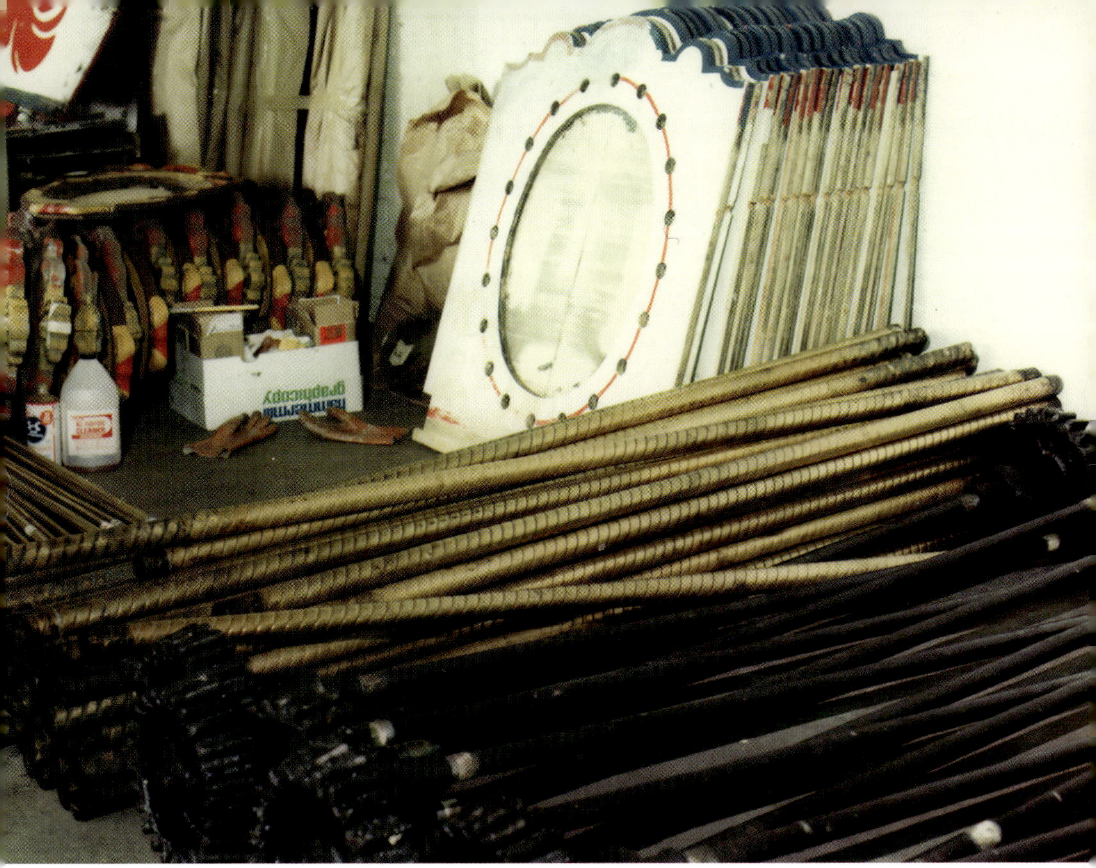

Mechanical and decorative parts were arrayed in a warehouse in spring 1990 for cleaning, repair, and restoration. Below, a nine-foot rounding board section waits to have its crown, drops, and lights removed. The original carved lion's head on this crown, destroyed by fire, was replaced with only a painting until volunteers gave it a new one.

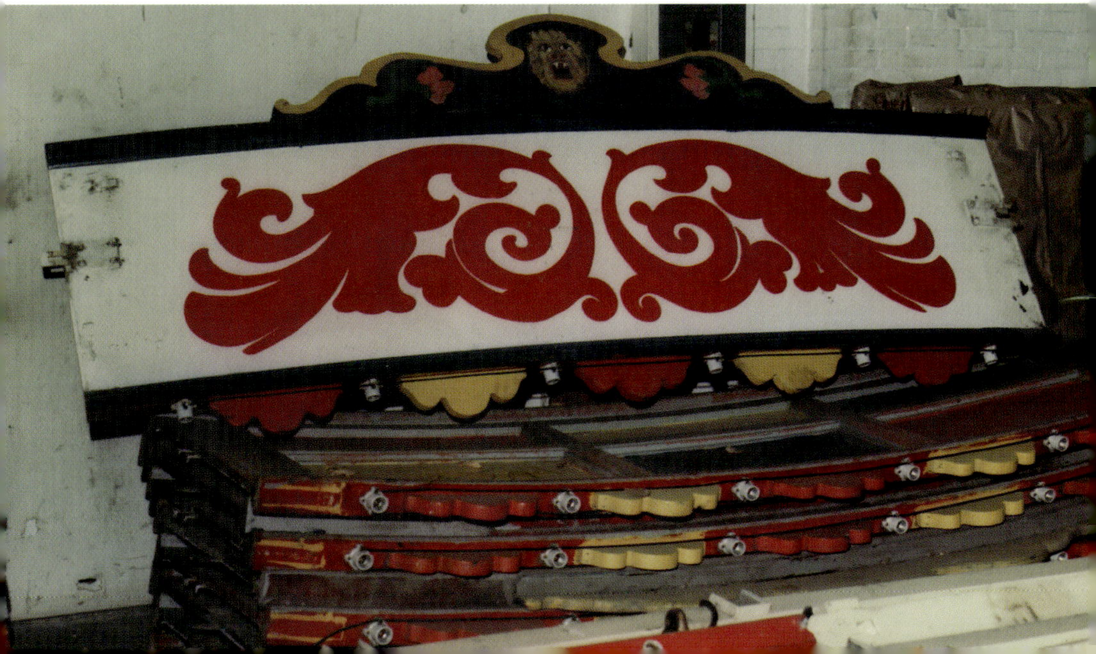

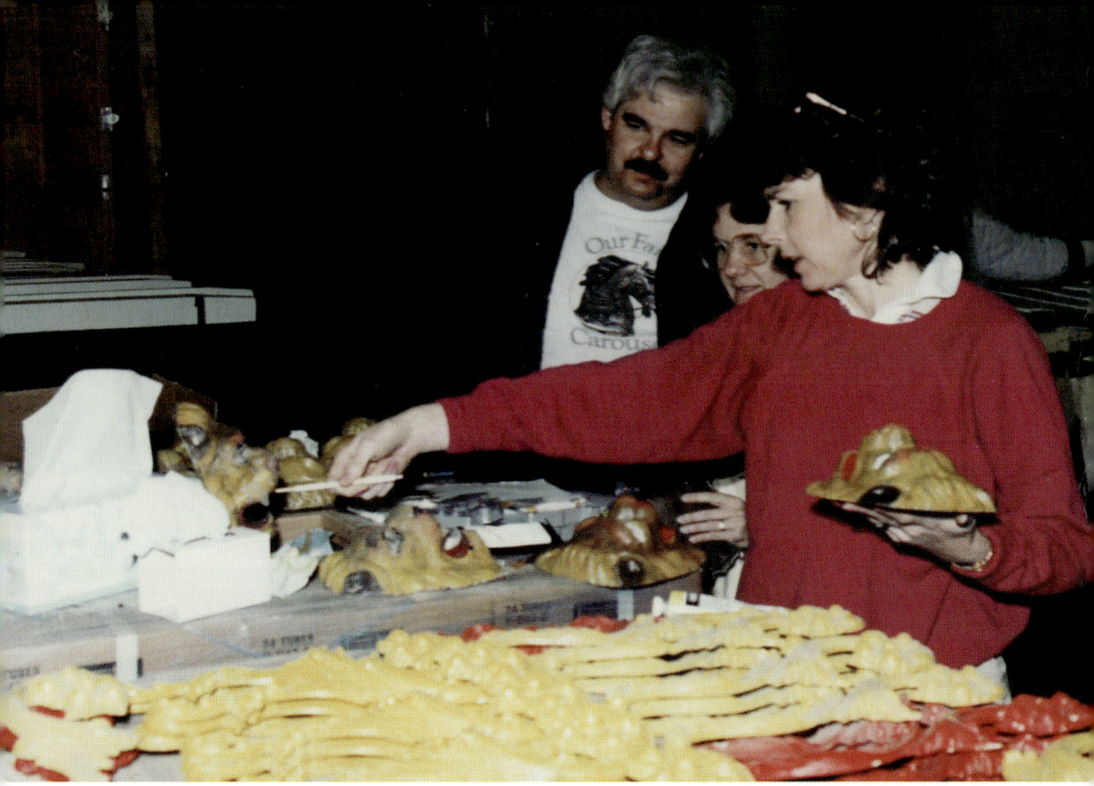

Peter listens as artists Jan Campbell and Carol Hegerman discuss the approach to repairing and repainting lions' heads. In the foreground are scrolls removed from mirror panels to be repainted and repaired. Behind the group, other artists apply stenciled patterns to the carousel's sweeps and spreaders. Below, Campbell works on a lion's head.

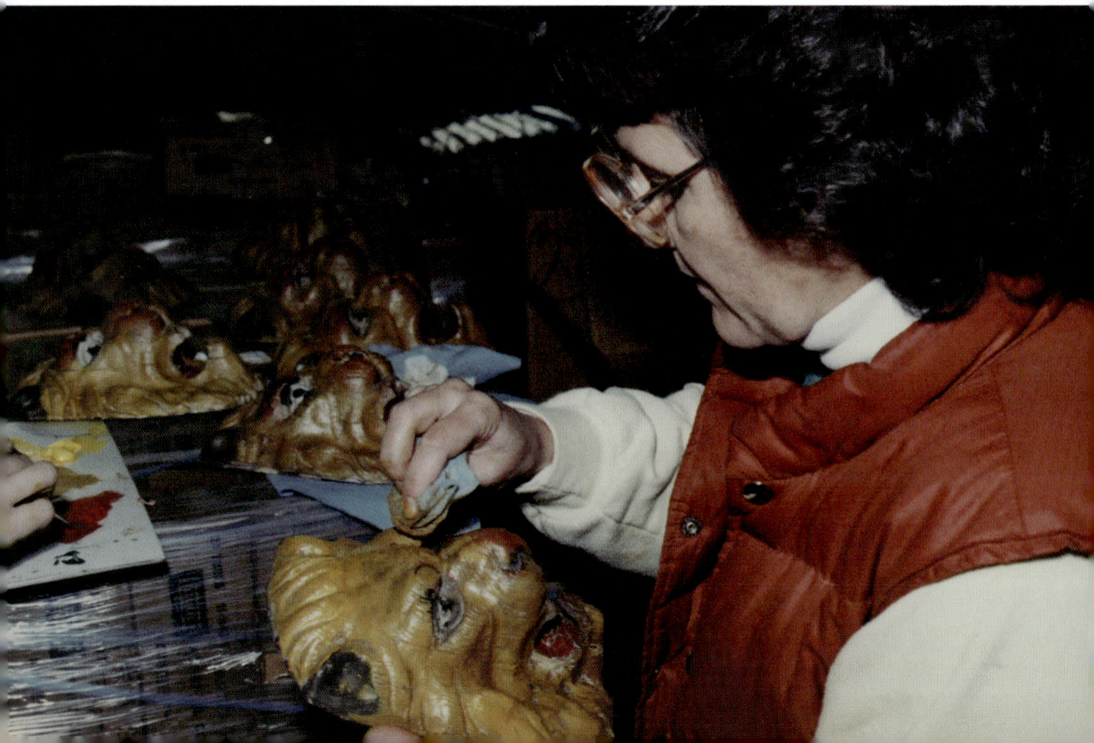

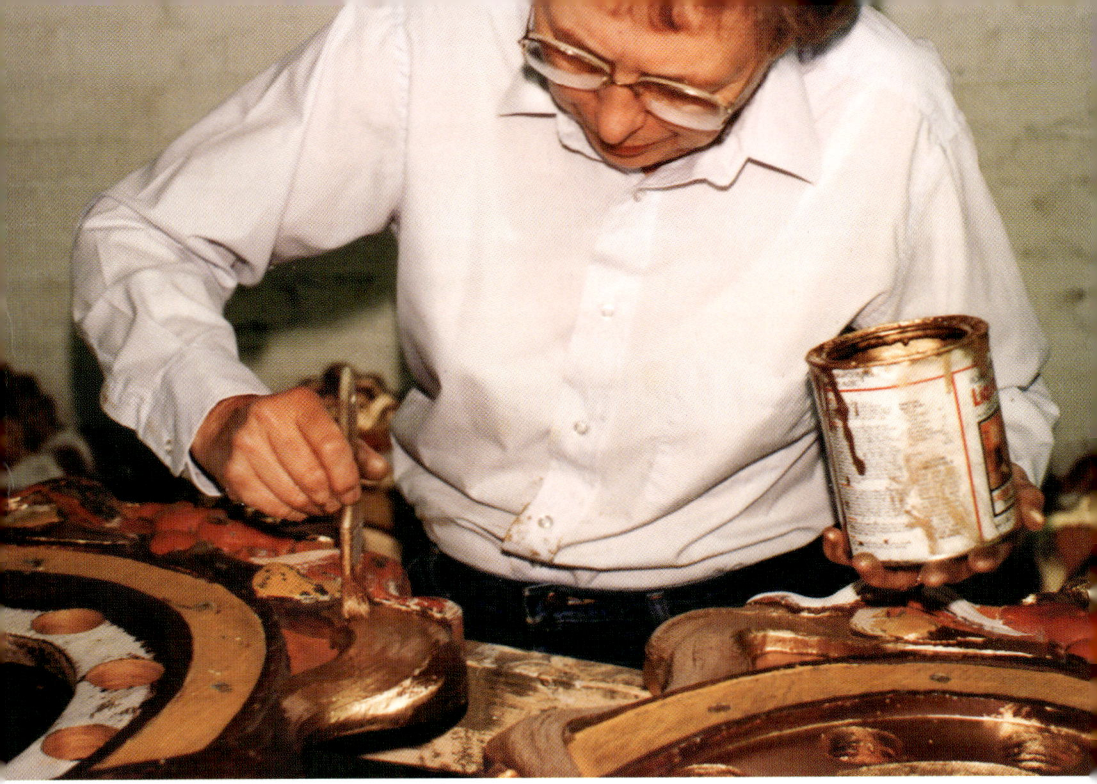

Where the carousel's rounding board sections meet hang 18 mirror shields, whose light sockets had been covered over after the 1939 fire. Artist Dodie Paul helps repaint the shields after we found traces of their original colors. The rounding board now extends below the shield because new wiring is concealed within an electrical box along the bottom of the section. *Bottom left photo by Robert Crump*

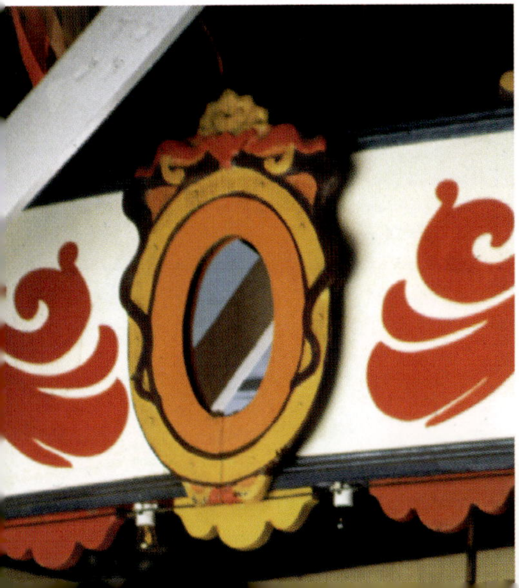

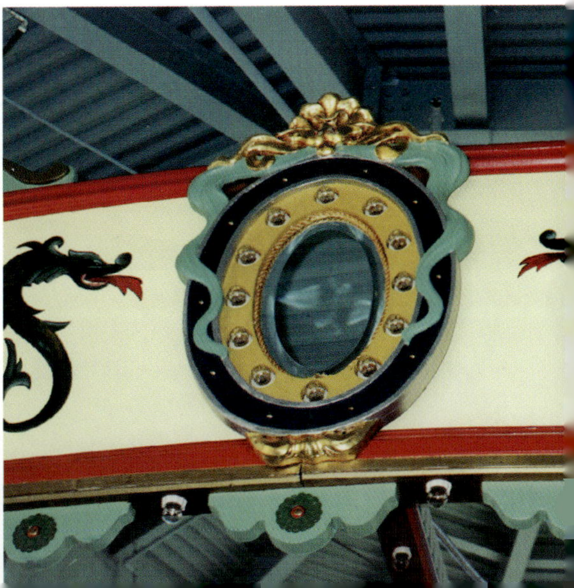

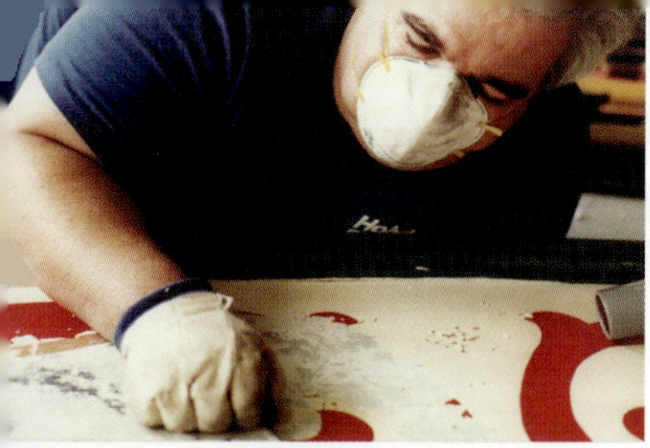

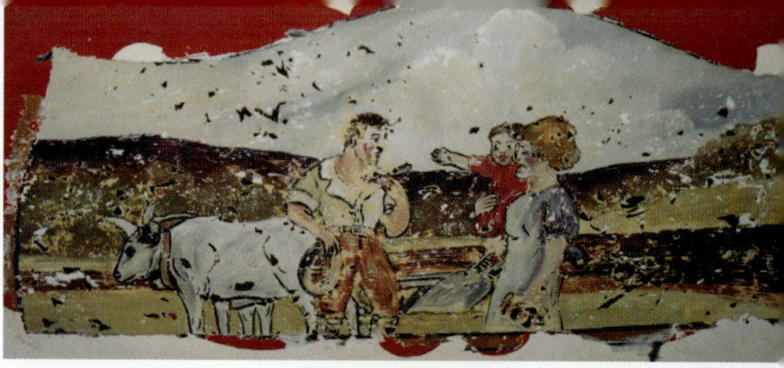

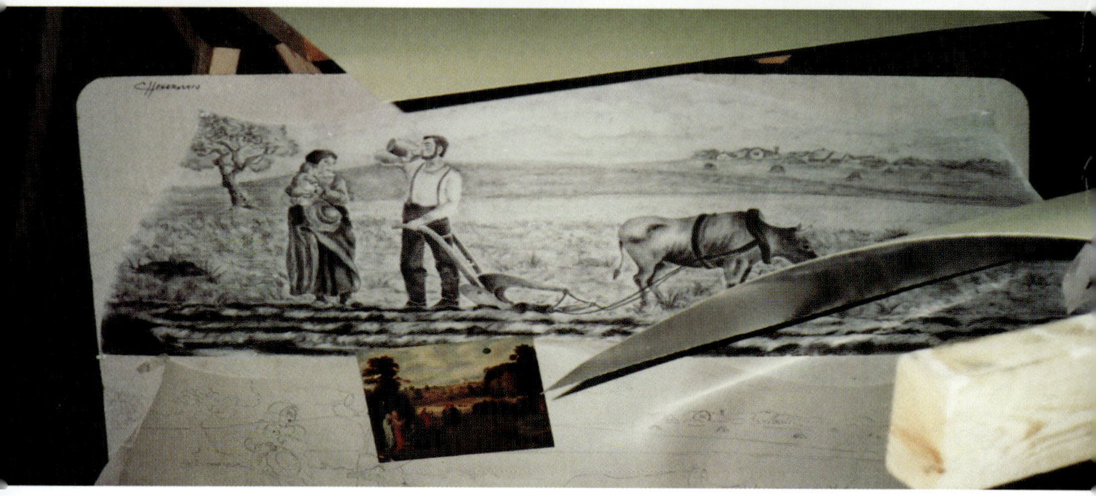

Under the red-and-white scroll on each rounding board segment, we unexpectedly found painted scenes applied after the 1939 fire destroyed the originals. We and other volunteers scraped away the red and white to reveal each scene. Then artist Carol Hegerman recreated the scene in a sketch in the style of Philadelphia Toboggan Company scene painter Max Soltmann, and volunteer artists painted the scenes on tin panels.

On the opposite page, a mill scene we uncovered, created by signpainters in 1939; artist Lucy Schneider creating a new scene with reference materials provided by Hegerman; the finished mill scene on Cafesjian's Carousel; and, at bottom, a Max Soltmann mill scene from PTC39 in Rossville, Georgia. *Bottom photo by Peter Boehm*

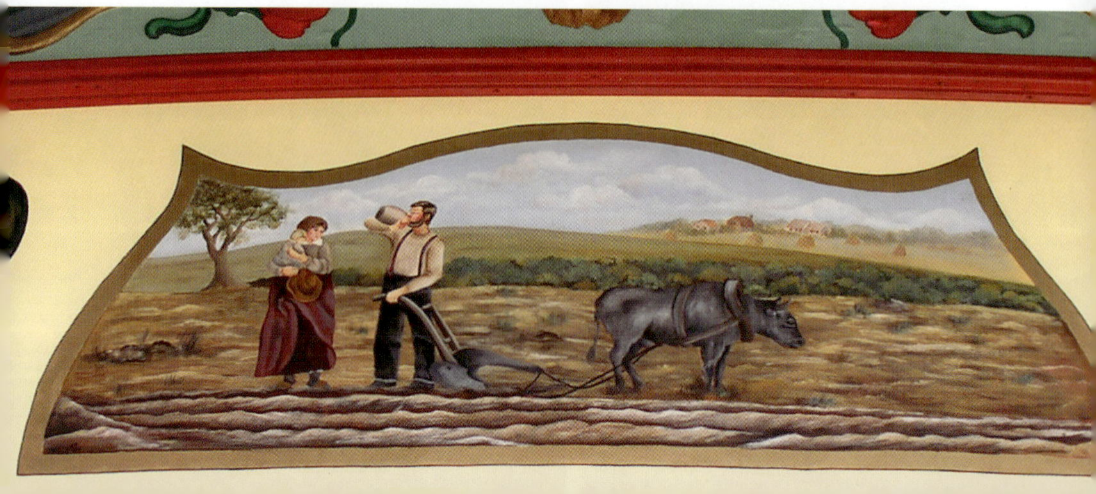

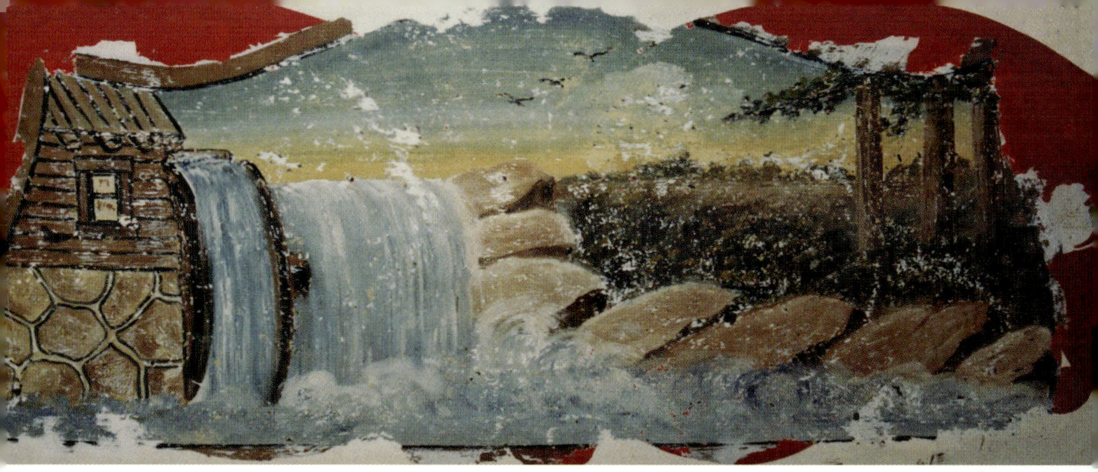

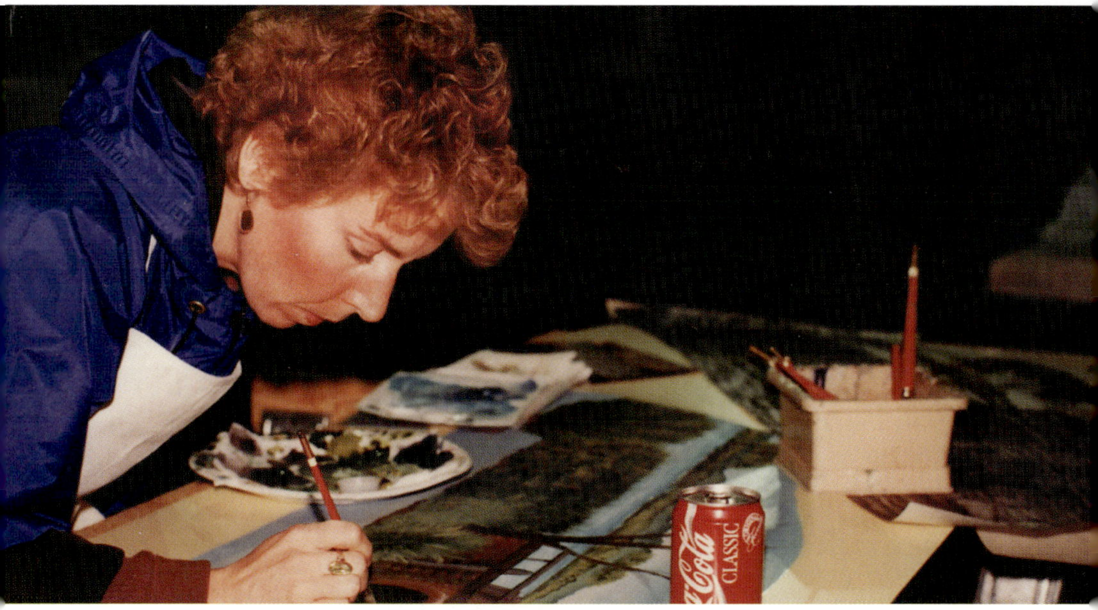
Coca-Cola
CLASSIC

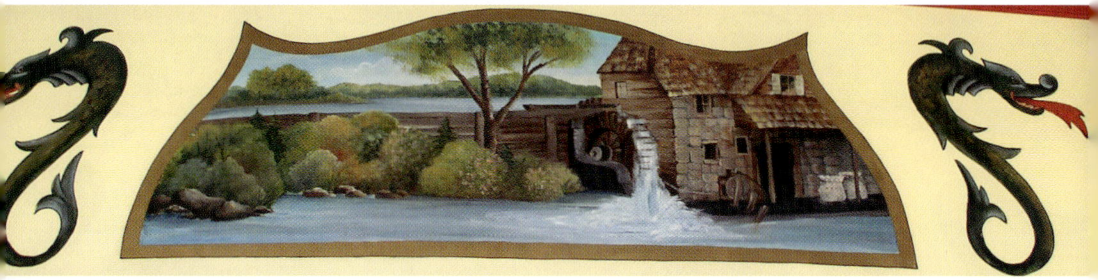

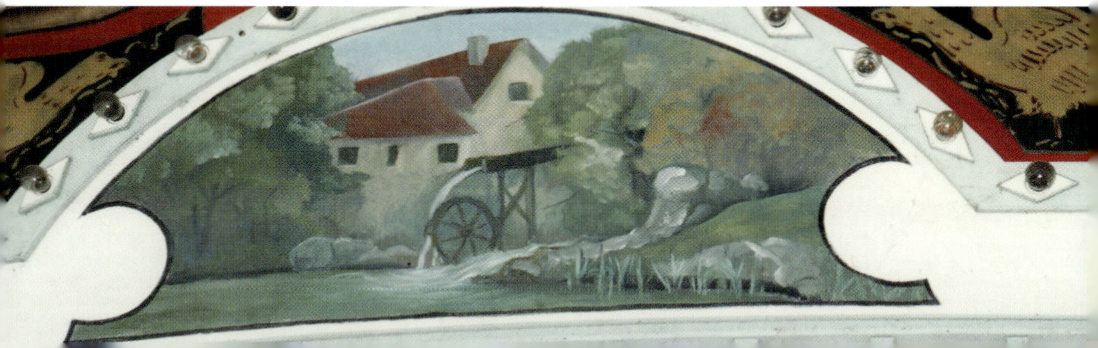

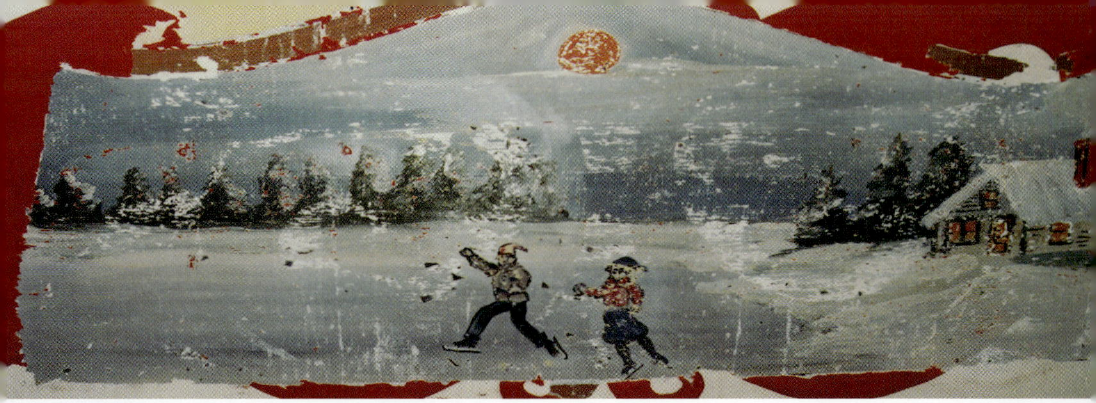

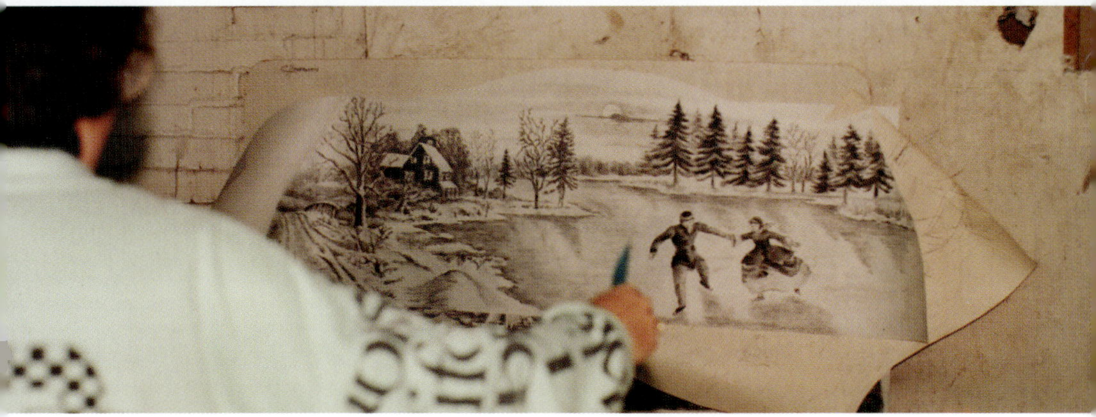

The scenes created for Cafesjian's Carousel all use the same themes as those found beneath the scrolls and are similar to scenes Soltmann painted on other PTC carousels.

To see all of the rounding board scene paintings visit www.ourfaircarousel.org.

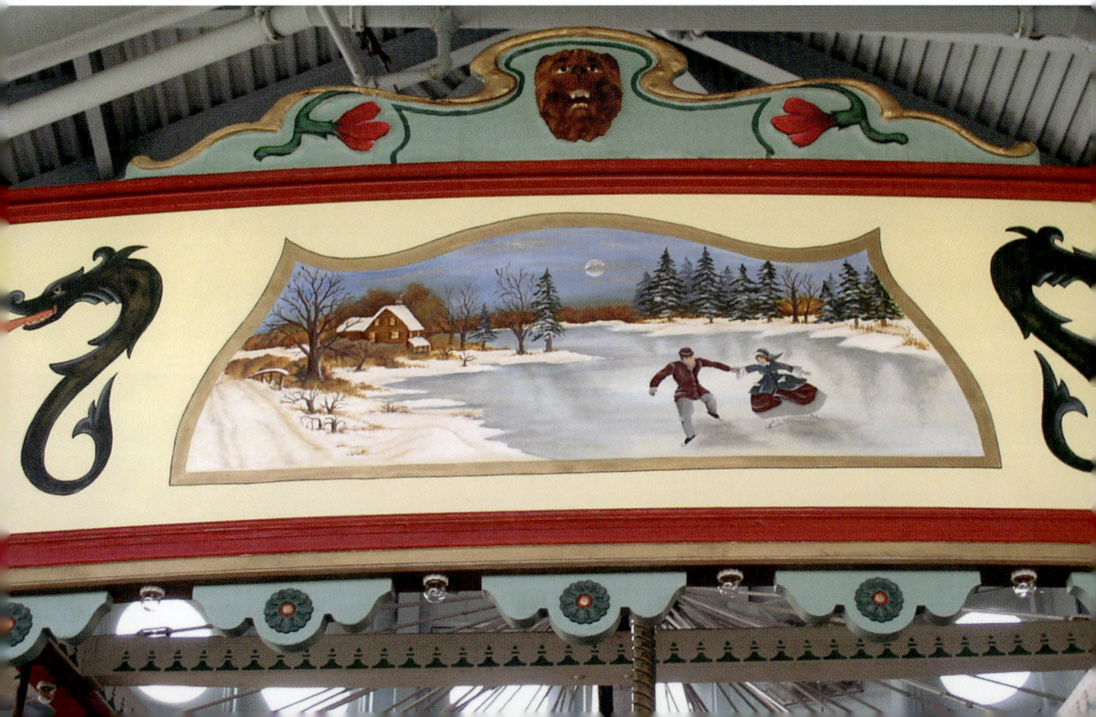

If you want to save a carousel, you'd better have a lot of money and power, or at least influential friends, right? In fact, it did take some well-positioned people to help get the job done, but we ourselves had neither wealth nor status. We were a working couple with modest income, living in a simple townhome in the Saint Paul suburb of Maplewood with Peter's 12-year-old daughter, Abby. We had met at a business meeting in April 1985 and married in September that same year. Nancy was director of publications and public relations at Macalester College, while Peter, a typesetter, had recently begun his own four-person company headquartered in the basement of our home. We both had been active in the community; Peter on the board of Children's Home Society and Nancy with the YWCA and as president of the professional group Women in Communications. It had been a year or two since we had done any projects with these groups, and Peter had recently been talking about finding a new way to volunteer in the community.

Like our marriage, our interest in carousels was relatively new. In summer 1987, in New Orleans for Peter's annual professional conference, Nancy noticed some carousel figurines in a gift shop on Royal Street. The personable saleslady said these figurines had become very popular; it was difficult to keep them in stock "If you like these, I have something else you should see," she said. She went into the back room and brought out a stunning picture book called *Painted Ponies,* Nancy's introduction to the world of carved carousel figures. Page after page of dramatic color photos showed beautiful wooden carousel figures, so much more striking than the little porcelain figures that had first caught her eye. She had to have that book. The store couldn't sell their only advance copy, so Nancy wrote down the title and authors (William Manns, Peggy Shank, and Marianne Stevens) and asked Peter to buy it for Christmas. In a time before Internet shopping, finding that book — so specialized, and brand new — was no easy task. But at Christmas it was gift-wrapped and under the tree.

The following summer the three of us — Peter, Nancy, and Abby — took a family vacation and drove to Peter's conference, this time

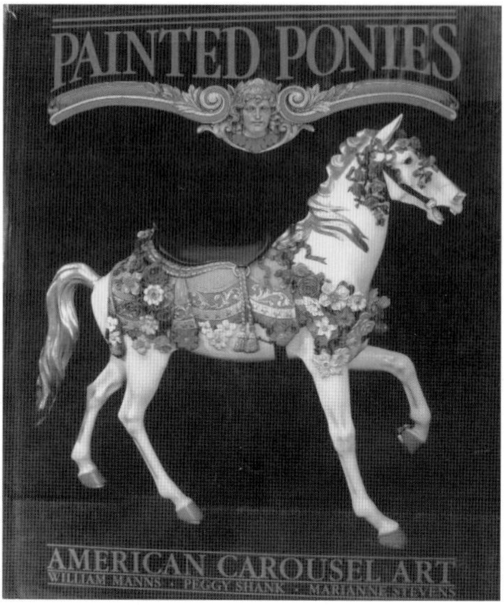

The book that changed our lives: The beautiful *Painted Ponies* by Marianne Stevens, Peggy Shank, and Bill Manns was a Christmas gift that became a well-worn travel guide that became a quarter-century commitment.

in Boston. To plan the trip, we tacked a map on a living room wall and for months we added Post-its for people and places we might want to visit. A list in *Painted Ponies* told us that eight of the best carousels in the country were on or near our route, so we added those to the itinerary. By the time we piled into the Mazda and hit the road, we had thoroughly overscheduled ourselves. For example, on Day 2 we would arrive in Chicago mid-morning to see a Georgia O'Keeffe exhibit and to meet up with Peter's old friend Marie and her husband. We joke that we told them to stand on the freeway overpass at 10 a.m. and we'd wave as we drove by, but in fact we met them on the steps of the Art Institute, they brought homemade muffins, and we had a great conversation that included some talk about our newfound interest in carousels. Leaving the museum we drove hard and fast to Adrian, Michigan, arriving two hours late for dinner with Nancy's college roommate Jan and her family. We had to leave their house early the next day so we could see three impressive carousels at Cedar Point near Sandusky, Ohio, and one at Conneaut Lake, Pennsylvania, and then on to our lodgings at...well, you get the idea.

Each time we drove toward another carousel, Nancy would pull out *Painted Ponies* and read aloud everything relevant to what we were going to see — the company that built it, who carved it and in what style, whether it had horses or menagerie animals. Sometimes there were before-and-after pictures of restored figures. Always there were pictures of the carousel we were seeing or others that were similar. Everything we now know about carousels we began learning on that trip by reading *Painted Ponies* and then examining — and riding — some wonderful old machines.

In late August, the three of us went to the Minnesota State Fair and rode what was billed as "The World's Largest Merry-Go-Round." It wasn't really the world's largest, but it was bigger and faster than most, and it ran more smoothly. Most important, the horses were lovely. We had seen more elaborate ones, for example on the Dentzel Kiddieland carousel at Cedar Point. But these seemed realistic, graceful, distinctive, and not at all pretentious. We were there in early evening and the place wasn't crowded, so we sat in a row of old-time theater chairs along one wall and watched the horses go around and around, up and down. We agreed that of all the carousels we'd visited this summer, we liked this one best. Wasn't it wonderful that it was right here where we lived, and that it belonged to the state fair so it would always be here! A month later we repeated this story to friends and family who had gathered at the home of Bill and Susan Schoenecker, Nancy's cousin and his wife. Many people there loved the carousel, too, and they were interested to learn that it compared so well with other, more celebrated carousels across the country. Weren't we lucky that it would be here for generations to come?

How little we knew.

Sheer luck — or was it fate? — conspired to get us involved in saving the carousel. On Saturday morning, November 12, 1988, we remained blissfully unaware of the previous day's *Star Tribune* story. Peter went out on a work-related errand, after which he planned to pick up supplies for a stained-glass art class he was taking. The job took longer than expected, and when he got to the glass shop just after noon, it had already closed. The day was cold and gloomy, and he wasn't going to be able to work on his glass project, so he stopped at the library to borrow a movie.

While Peter was gone, Nancy got a call from Susan Schoenecker, who asked what we knew about the state fair carousel being sold. Susan's sister Kathleen Paul was among those at the party who had talked with us about carousels. Kathleen had read the *Star Tribune* story, and on Saturday she called Susan. "I'm so upset I couldn't sleep last night. And then I thought that if anybody knows what to do, it's Peter and Nancy."

A few minutes later, Peter called from the library and Nancy repeated the conversation. We laughed at Kathleen's faith in us, and then decided we should find out what was in the story. "I'm right here at the library," Peter said "I'll make a copy." He came home with the story and a movie. Whatever the movie was, we never got around to watching it.

All afternoon we read the story again and again. We went away and did other things and returned to the story. Our discussion moved from "How can this be?" to "Who can we think of that could save it?" to "What can *we* do?" We kept coming back to the fact that if we felt so strongly, and Kathleen felt so strongly, then other people did, too. Like us, those other people didn't know where to turn, what to do. At the same time, we thought that if someone with resources — a business, a foundation, a government agency, a preservation group — saw an outpouring of community support, they just might be motivated to step in and do something heroic.

We decided that we could step forward and be a focal point for people to voice their support for the carousel. We would invite them to contact us, and to send small contributions if they wished. At the same time we would be a point of connection, a clearinghouse, for anyone with an active interest and, we hoped, the kinds of resources needed to save the carousel.

Over dinner we continued to talk. Nancy pictured our role as finding an organization to take over the carousel, to safeguard and operate it. Peter said the owner had tried and failed to find a buyer. We weren't likely to find a group sitting on an extra million dollars or being able to add a carousel to its mission. The only way to get the job done, he said, was for us to purchase and run the carousel through a nonprofit organization. To Nancy, that sounded impossibly challenging. She thought, "Who are we to even consider this?" Peter, on the other hand, called on a favorite motto: "What's the worst that can happen?" His answer: "If we fail, the carousel gets sold but at least we gave it our best. If we don't even try, it gets sold and we always wonder whether we could have saved it."

We assessed the skills we could bring to the effort. Peter was great at tracking down information by phone, which would be critical. He wasn't shy, he could always marshal a good argument, and he could be very persuasive. He owned his own business and worked from home, so he could set his own schedule. If he needed to be available for the carousel during the day, he could do his work at night. Nancy had a good sense of who was who among community leaders, and she knew how to give media people what they needed in order to cover a story. When Peter finally asked, "Should we try this?" Nancy said, "Sure."

Did we have any idea what we were getting into? Of course not. If we had known – about all the work and worry and sleepless nights – maybe we'd have watched that movie instead of making phone calls. Or maybe this was something we were meant to do together.

The *Star Tribune* story identified the carousel's owner as William Blinstrup of Eden Prairie, so Peter looked him up in the phone book and called. Blinstrup seemed distant when he first answered the phone. People had been calling for two days, berating him for breaking up the carousel. But he relaxed a bit when Peter said, "If you're going to sell, I want to figure out how to be the guy who buys the whole thing." Blinstrup said we would have to make a written offer and have it accepted before the first horse was sold at auction. The minimum opening bid was $1.08 million. "But that's no guarantee," Peter said. "A group with more money could outbid us." True, Blinstrup replied, but the family would prefer to sell to someone who would keep the carousel operating in the Twin Cities. When Peter hung up, he said with a straight face, "Nothing to it, we just have to come up with a little over a million dollars in the next four weeks."

We spent the rest of Saturday evening leaving messages for people who weren't in. We tried Barbara Flanagan, long-time *Star Tribune* columnist who had often advocated a carousel as part of city beautification. We left a message for Karal Ann Marling, a University of Minnesota art historian with a special interest in the state fair. We left a message for someone Nancy knew in the governor's office. We called Nancy Loucks, editor of *Carousel News & Trader*, who had been quoted in the *Star Tribune* story. She was away from her Michigan home for the weekend, but she called back Sunday evening and gave us valuable background as well as names of people active in the National Carousel Association whose advice would prove useful.

On Sunday Bill and Susan came over to help us outline a business plan. We would form a nonprofit organization called Our Fair Carousel. Its mission: to purchase, maintain, and restore antique carousels and operate them for the public. (Yes, we said "carousels" just in case an opportunity came along to help save more than one.) We would open a bank account and a post office box immediately. We talked about a "public-private partnership." We needed a larger, more established organization to help us with funding, and we thought the best approach would be to forge a partnership with a governmental unit — a city, a county, or the state — that could help us get a loan and maybe provide a site for the carousel after it left the fair. To help with fundraising we would create an Adopt-a-Pony plan recognizing gifts of $5,000 to $25,000. We agreed to hold a press conference to take these plans public; we thought Thursday morning was the earliest we could be ready. On Monday Bill filed incorporation papers at the Secretary of State's office while Peter went to the bank and the post office and continued to work the phone.

Saint Paul *Pioneer Press* columnist Nick Coleman was calling around town on Monday for a Tuesday morning piece about the loss of the ride. Coleman talked with Karal Ann Marling, who said she hadn't been following the story but had gotten several phone messages about it. Coleman took Peter's name and number and called to interview him. In his piece, Coleman wrote of watching his own children ride at the fair. "From the time my girl disappears in a blur until she comes out of the whirl again, it is only 10 seconds — a mere flash for such an immense planet to turn in its orbit." He chastised the state fair board for having demonstrated "little creativity" in striving for the carousel's survival. "Next month," he wrote, "it will be on a New York City auction block and rich people will pay $30,000 or more for the hand-carved horses, taking pieces of a charmed carousel for their dens."

Katy Frantz, whose great-grandfather Clarke Chambers was a co-founder of the fair, echoed the theme. "To me, the carousel is the heart and soul of the state fair," she told Coleman. "Generations have ridden on that carousel. Why do they have to sell it off to the fat cats in Manhattan?" She and her husband had watched their kids ride and still returned to watch others. "What a wonderful, unifying thing it is," she said. "Whether you're a Democrat or a Republican, black or white, 3 or 93, it's one of the few things that connects everybody."

Coleman reported that we were setting up a nonprofit corporation to try to preserve the carousel. "They are hoping some philanthropist or foundation will come forward to help," he wrote. "If not, they are hoping the public will get into the act." Near the end of his column he said, "If you want to help, you can call Peter Boehm," and he listed our telephone number.

The newspaper containing that column was still on our doorstep and we were still asleep Tuesday, November 15, when our phone rang just after 6 a.m. It was Nancy's early-rising friend Carol Kerner, calling to say that our number was being given out repeatedly on radio station KSTP's popular morning show. Chuck Knapp and Michael "Donuts" Douglas were reading Coleman's column on air and doing their best to move their listeners to action. They repeated our telephone number often. A public relations professional, Carol knew the value of this exposure. "You'd better put on some coffee and be ready to answer the phone," she said.

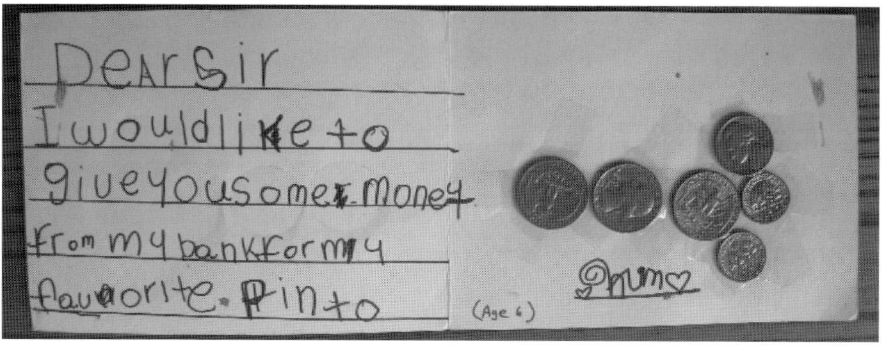

This is one of our our favorite contributions. Six-year-old Kim Taylor's coins became an iconic story that we used in talks and media interviews to illustrate the community's heartfelt support for the carousel.

We jumped up and got dressed, but the phone was silent. We began to worry that we'd been wrong, that nobody cared. But true to their nature, Minnesotans were just being polite. By 8 a.m. the phone was ringing constantly, and it didn't stop for three days. Many callers told sweet stories about their families riding the carousel for generations. Some wanted to rant about the state fair's decision; we told them we thought it was futile to try to change the board's mind and therefore we had a new plan. Some had suggestions: "You should get an injunction to stop the sale," or "If every school child in Minnesota gave a dollar...." Throughout these conversations the second incoming line would click, letting us know another caller was trying to get through. Whichever of us was taking the call would interrupt the conversation, jot down the second caller's name and number, and hand it off to the other person to call back using Peter's business line. Even with two conversations going at all times, we sometimes had a dozen names waiting to be called back.

The carousel had been the scene of first dates, engagements, wedding photos, birthday rides, annual end-of-summer treats, and multi-generation traditions. Soft-spoken Arthur Rusterholz was a great example. "I'm 76 years old," he told us. "Seventy years ago my father hoisted me up onto the Indian pony, right in front of the horse with the alligator on its saddle. I've ridden that horse every year since, and I've put my children and grandchildren on it." We began asking our callers to write down their stories and send them to us. In the following weeks and months those stories of innocence and families and generations helped us make our case again and again.

We invited people to send checks, and many did so — mostly $5 and $10, but sometimes $100. We were touched that people were so trusting, and pleased because this was further evidence that the carousel mattered.

Over the weekend, while we had been deciding to get involved, a Saint Paul City Council member was doing the same. Tom Dimond was interested in historic preservation and saw the carousel as a potential attraction for a riverfront park on Harriet Island, just across the Mississippi from downtown. He and his staff spent Monday making calls to Blinstrup, the auction house, and people within city government. Dimond wanted the city to buy and operate the carousel. As he called various city departments he found some interest, but also many questions about how and whether the city should get involved.

On Tuesday morning, while we were immersed in our first wave of phone calls, Dimond and fellow council member Jim Scheibel floated an idea at a council meeting: the city could pay half the cost to buy the carousel if an individual or organization came up with the other half. Dimond had talked with Guernsey's president Arlan Ettinger, who reiterated that a bid of $1.08 million would keep the carousel intact but that competing bids from other parties would then be allowed. Then Ettinger, by all accounts a skilled negotiator, said he would give Saint Paul special consideration: For $1.5 million Ettinger would pull the carousel out of the auction and allow the city to buy it outright. Dimond wanted to go forward immediately. Funds were earmarked for improvements at Harriett Island, and he proposed using some of those to buy the carousel and place it there. Council members expressed cautious optimism. Mayor George Latimer put in an appearance to say he liked the idea of keeping the carousel in Saint Paul but cautioned about spending public funds. The *Pioneer Press* quoted him telling the council, "It's a lot of money. We should think a while about whether this is deserving of a budgetary outlay." Dimond and others promised to bring in proposed legislation at the council's next meeting in two days.

We were excited to learn of Tom Dimond's interest, and Peter quickly called to talk about our mutual interests. Like him, we wanted to save the carousel, and we agreed that a Saint Paul park would be an ideal location. But Harriet Island was on a flood plain, and floods had destroyed many of the country's antique carousels. It became clear that Dimond wanted the city to own and operate the carousel. We thought that was not the best use of taxpayers' money, and we felt that city ownership might not protect and preserve the carousel. From our perspective, Dimond's plan was not the answer, but the council's considerations opened the door to the kind of partnership we had envisioned.

Thursday, November 17, was the day we had planned to introduce Our Fair Carousel to the community through a news conference. There was no need; because of Nick Coleman's column we were being covered by both daily newspapers, broadcast media were picking up the story, and the *Pioneer Press* was even running a box telling people how to send us donations. On the other hand, with the city council taking up Tom Dimond's proposal that day, Thursday's *Pioneer Press* included an editorial and a second Nick Coleman column, both endorsing the Dimond plan. To move forward, we didn't need publicity; we needed to be at the negotiating table.

We attended the city council meeting prepared to make our case. About a dozen carousel fans — none of whom we had met before but several of whom became valued volunteers — sat in the council chambers' gallery. We were excited and nervous. When the time came, Dimond presented his proposal that the city buy the carousel outright and then seek private funds over the coming year to cover the costs. During discussion, council member Bob Long introduced some amendments defining funding sources, which were accepted. When citizens were invited to speak, Peter talked about Our Fair Carousel and others talked about why saving the carousel was the right thing to do. They almost needn't have bothered, because council members themselves, some of whom wore "Save the Carousel" buttons provided by Dimond's staff, had a lot to say on the subject, and nobody spoke against it.

Before the vote there was a memorable bit of theatrics. As Tom Dimond's aide Dave Thune was preparing for this meeting, he had received a call from a man who offered images of carousel riders at the state fair over the years. Thune drove some distance to meet the man, wondering whether the trek would be worthwhile. Sorting the images the night before the meeting, he knew that it was. Pictured among the riders were council member Kiki Sonnen and her husband Sammy on their favorite horses. As Thune advanced the slides during the meeting, shouts suddenly went up around the council table. "It's Kiki!" "It's Sammy!" We let out a sigh of relief. Council members would never be this animated if they planned to vote against saving the carousel. The vote was taken: 6 ayes and 0 nays. The gallery applauded loud and long, and council members looked pleased. A jubilant Tom Dimond called the vote "Saint Paul's Christmas present to Saint Paul."

Media reports all led with the headline that the council had voted to buy the carousel. But remember those amendments that Bob Long had proposed, and that the council had quietly accepted? One of them provided that the city could use its reserve funds to guarantee a bank loan for a community group, rather than the city itself, to buy the carousel. Nobody made an issue of it during the meeting, and the casual observer might not have noticed, but we did. We used our presence at the meeting to let council members know that we stood ready to be that community group. Peter made that the focus of his presentation, and Nancy had quietly placed an OFC fact sheet at each council member's place.

When the council voted, Tom Dimond perceived it as approval of his preferred plan, and he told reporters that the city would be in touch with the carousel's owners immediately to get the purchase underway. He would soon learn that people in city hall had other ideas.

Within a couple of hours council member Bill Wilson was scuttling the plan. Wilson, who had voted for Dimond's proposal, told a *Pioneer Press* reporter that he had second thoughts and would ask the council to reconsider. "It's too risky, too expensive, and there are not enough reassurances," he said. Wilson pointed out that Saint Paul had recently found it difficult to raise $1 million to refurbish the 70-year-old conservatory at the city's popular Como Park. Mayor Latimer, who had seemed to bless the idea in the morning, now threatened to veto it, though he promised to wait five days before deciding. Both announcements served notice to Tom Dimond that his plan was at risk. He had not seen this coming and he was upset. But Wilson and Latimer had created a four-day window to work out a compromise.

At home early that afternoon, we got a call from David Lanegran, a Macalester College professor who was at the heart of Saint Paul's historic preservation activities. When we decided to rescue the carousel, he was the first person Nancy had called for advice about preservation and about navigating the political process. Now he was calling with timely, urgent news of Bill Wilson's announcement and Dimond's angry response. Lanegran predicted that if things continued along this path and Wilson reintroduced the issue at the next council meeting, the entire deal could fall apart. He urged Peter to call Bob Long and ask that Long, as a neutral party, convene a meeting that would bring Dimond, Wilson, Peter, and the mayor's office to the negotiating table.

We had developed the habit of jotting down talking points before an important phone conversation. When Peter called Bob Long, he had four notes. First, he said we were very sympathetic to Long's amendment that would have a community group purchasing the carousel, and we stood ready to be that group. Second, Peter said city ownership was likely to create problems for fundraising. Preservationists might worry that the city would not take good care of the carousel. "They picture a park employee slapping a coat of paint on it," he said, bluntly describing what had happened to carousels elsewhere. Meanwhile there would be a continuing outcry from people who opposed the use of city funds in the first place. Third, the situation called for someone to mediate a solution. Finally, he said Lanegran had suggested asking Long to play that role. Long set a meeting for the next morning.

At the meeting, Peter repeated the points he had made to Long the previous afternoon. Wilson said he favored having the city act as a guarantor of a bank loan to a community group. He thought maybe the carousel's new owner would be able to keep it at the state fair. Long agreed with Dimond that the carousel should be in Saint Paul, which the fair is not, but said it would take more information to decide on a specific location. Peter said the city should not yet be negotiating terms with the owners or the auction house; he was confident a better deal could be made than the $1.5 million Dimond was proposing to pay. Dimond made no concessions. He clearly believed the city had a better chance of success than we did, and he was afraid that if we were allowed into the process the carousel would be lost. Frankly, given that we were unknowns, the others had to be wondering, too. Finally, the group asked both Peter and Tom Dimond to bring written proposals to what would be a decisive meeting early Monday morning.

We spent the weekend writing and polishing a business plan, building on the ideas we had laid out the previous Sunday and incorporating plenty of detail based on conversations we'd had all week with carousel experts. We said the not-for-profit Our Fair Carousel would operate the carousel on a self-sustaining basis using volunteer staffing. The city would provide an appropriate space; we outlined criteria for site selection, including protection from floods. We described plans to restore the carousel's valuable old paint to maximize its future value. We built a budget showing it would cost $1.25 million to purchase the carousel and return the horses to the Twin Cities and we itemized other costs that would be incurred before the carousel could operate again. We outlined our Adopt-A-Pony fundraising plan for major gifts, discussed the value of small gifts from a broad base, and said we hoped to be allowed to operate at the 1989 state fair, selling t-shirts and buttons to raise funds and awareness. We said OFC should lead the fundraising, and the city should avoid confusing potential donors.

For example, we noted that the city had established its own fund for donor gifts, the address for which now appeared alongside ours in the *Pioneer Press*.

Finally, to underscore the community-wide effort that we envisioned, we described the board of directors we intended to assemble, including business leaders, preservation experts, knowledgeable carousel enthusiasts, and city representatives. The board would be responsible for raising more than a million dollars to repay the loan within one year. We acknowledged that if OFC failed, the city would be free to sell the carousel to recover the funds. This business plan was our first important project together, and our skills meshed perfectly: it read well, looked good, and presented a substantive vision for acquiring and operating the carousel. When Peter walked into that crucial meeting Monday morning, he felt prepared. When he saw Tom Dimond's single sheet with five or six bullet points, he felt confident. And he knew one more thing.

As soon as media had announced the council's vote to buy the carousel, city hall began to get calls from people who thought Saint Paul had better uses for its funds. We had predicted this, but we left nothing to chance. We had pages of callers' names and numbers, and most had said "Let me know how I can help." So before starting work on our business plan we enlisted a handful of people to contact the others with a simple message: Tell the city they should not buy the carousel but should help OFC to do so. A week earlier, most callers seemed ready to support anything the city would do to save the doomed carousel. By Monday morning the climate had changed, and everyone, including Tom Dimond, could feel it.

At that Monday meeting Peter emphasized that in our plan city reserves would be tied up for a year but would never really be at risk. Our Fair Carousel would bear all responsibility for repaying the loan, either with fundraising or by handing over the carousel for the city to sell. This was the solution Wilson and Long had wanted, and a plan the mayor could support. They told Tom Dimond this was the only way to keep the carousel in Saint Paul.

He agreed to present this new, restructured proposal at the next day's council meeting.

While Peter was still at city hall, he got word that Mayor Latimer wanted to see us. Nancy hurried from work for the 11:30 meeting. The mayor introduced us to Joe Franzgrote, president of the local NBC affiliate which had recently changed its call letters to KARE. Franzgrote said KARE would provide $250,000 in public-service air time and production assistance to promote the carousel's fund-raising efforts over a two-year period. In exchange, he wanted us to rename it the KARE-ousel. We hesitated, each of us silently considering the implications of this offer. Then we politely thanked Franzgrote and said we needed to focus first on the purchase and after that we could think about how the offer would fit with our fundraising plans. The mayor replied, as tactfully as he could, that we were an unknown quantity and a deal like this would give us some much-needed credibility. He implied, if he didn't say, that we needed to accept this offer to ensure the city's partnership. We smiled and said thanks. That evening we wrote and distributed a news release alerting the media to expect a new action from the city council.

So there we were on Tuesday, November 22, back in the city council's chambers as they discussed a new carousel proposal. Abby came along to watch what we considered a significant civics lesson. In the new plan, the Parks and Recreation Department would create a partnership with Our Fair Carousel. The city would transfer $1.3 million from its reserve funds to the Parks and Recreation budget, to be held there as backing for a bank loan to OFC. When the council approved the measure, we had the "public-private partnership" we could only imagine 10 days earlier. Peter took the floor to thank the council. Then, as the mayor had asked, he announced the offer from KARE TV. Council member Jim Scheibel quipped, "I predict it's going to be named 'Karousel' with a K."

We were surrounded by reporters as we left the meeting, and we told each of them the same thing: The carousel was not yet saved. We had 18 days to negotiate its purchase and get a loan.

After that, we would have a single year to raise more than a million dollars. Only then would it be secure. We did a television interview on the sunny sidewalk outside City Hall, and then we drove to Minneapolis where Nancy did a live interview on WCCO television's noon news.

Two days later was Thanksgiving. Our heads were spinning as we celebrated the holiday. We received a call from downtown promoter and dealmaker Ron Maddox, a colorful character, former city council member, and operator of Taste of Minnesota. He invited us to a Friday lunch with him and businessman Bob Angleson, who headed local operations for BCED, a company that owned a downtown building called Town Square. Maddox began the conversation with a lame off-color joke. We didn't laugh.

Angleson moved quickly to the purpose of the meeting. Town Square had a mix of retail shops and a food court, and it was connected by skyway to Dayton's and virtually everything else that brought people downtown. Atop the building, reached by escalator and elevator, was an indoor park under a glass ceiling. What we didn't know until then was that Town Square Park was part of the city's park system. Angleson suggested that it would make an ideal home for the carousel. It would be secure, we could operate year-round, and because BCED already had a budget for renovations there would be no cost to us or the city. The only question would be whether the site was large enough; it would be a close fit at best.

It was a genuinely interesting proposal, and we said so. We preferred Como Park, a large and busy place that would provide a beautiful setting and, we assumed, a ready stream of riders. But the city considered Como to be overused. Besides, any outdoor park would require a new building and we didn't know how that would be paid for. We thanked Angleson and said we'd get back to him once we actually owned the carousel. That's when Ron Maddox said, "You two have done a great job of getting the carousel to this point. Now you should step back and let the people who know the players get the rest of the job done."

Suddenly things fell into place. Nancy surmised that Maddox hoped Angleson would pay him to arrange the details and maybe operate the carousel. Initially, she had hoped we could find someone who would do just that. But hearing Maddox's suggestion, she realized she was ready to battle anybody who tried to push us aside. Her eyes flashed, but she held her tongue. Peter simply chuckled and said, "It looks to me like we're sitting with the players. I think we can find them, and they can find us."

That afternoon *Pioneer Press* reporter Les Suzukamo called to verify that we had spoken with Angleson. Peter said yes, we had heard his proposal and we weren't ruling it out. We expected a small story, maybe a couple of inches on an inside page. Instead, on Saturday morning we found a page-wide headline atop the local section announcing "Town Square an option for carousel." The story reported, "Over a pasta lunch at Spazzo's restaurant in Town Center, adjacent to Town Square, [OFC] and [BCED] officials talked turkey about relocating the carousel to Town Square." It quoted Angleson at some length about the site's advantages.

We laughed. Two weeks earlier, we'd been an anonymous suburban couple. This day, the paper was reporting where and with whom we'd had lunch. Clearly, the carousel saga was a big story.

For the next three weeks, carousel stories ran in both newspapers—nearly every day—often on page one or the first page of the metro section. Television and radio reported the story as well, sometimes from wire service reports but usually from interviewing us.

We had begun our project thinking that Nancy would speak for us in the media because of her public relations background. But from the day Nick Coleman first called and launched us into the media, it was Peter who was reachable virtually any time of day. He found it easy to give interviews by phone or in person; he was never nervous and always had all the facts clearly in mind. That became clear in the first week of our involvement when we got a 6 a.m. call from WCCO radio newsman Eric Eskola. "What do you have against free enterprise?" Eskola asked, on-air. Peter, awakened by the phone, didn't miss a beat. He replied, matter-of-factly,

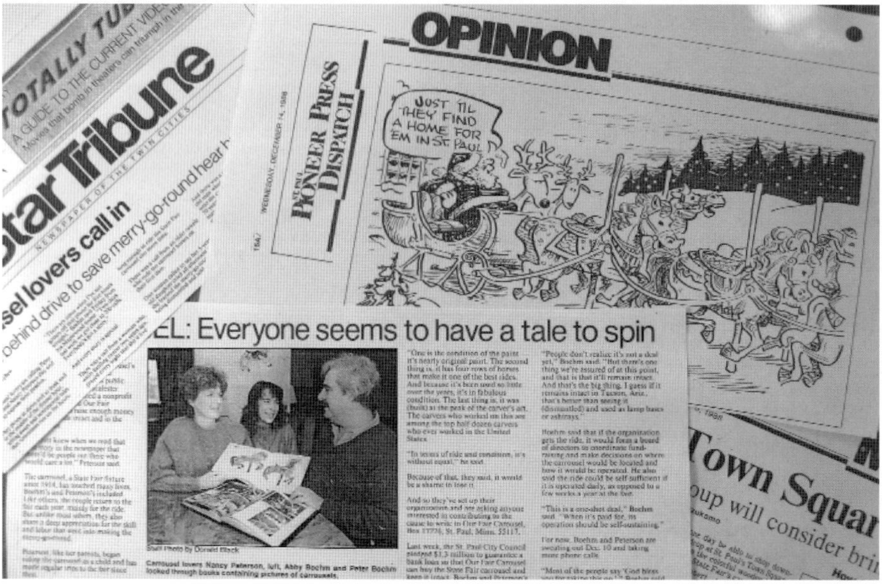

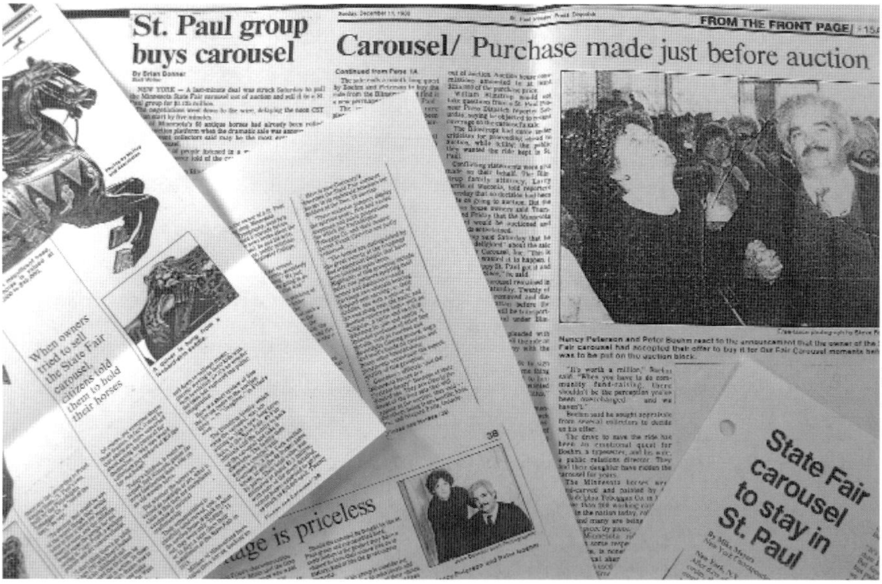

The community's effort to save a beloved and endangered carousel drew significant media attention; these are just a few of the clippings from that month.

"I have nothing against free enterprise. Someone who owns a carousel is free to sell it. I just want to be the guy who buys it."

Nancy, on the other hand, realized that she never liked appearing in the media; her job had always involved crafting messages to be delivered by others. While her live television news interview had gone fine, she found it nerve-wracking and draining. It made sense for her to work on strategy and for Peter to be our spokesperson. He was a quick study. Watching television coverage of the day he first spoke before the city council, he had one question: "The stories include visuals of me speaking, but why didn't they use any of what I said?" There had been snippets of others, including Saint Paul mom Barbara McCormick who held her toddler son and urged the council to keep the carousel available for him to ride. Nancy instantly recognized the problem. "I wrote you a speech aimed at the city council," she said, "but I didn't give you any sound bites." A sound bite, she explained, is a colorful sentence that summarizes your point. "The shorter and more memorable, the more likely the media will use it," she said. She paused to think of an example from the day's news. "Oh, you mean like this?" Peter said, and he rattled off two or three examples. He never again had trouble getting quoted.

It became our morning routine to talk a few minutes to prepare for the day's media activity. What information do we want to communicate today, and what is our key message? The two are not always the same. Reporters were calling for updates on our progress toward the purchase, and we provided each incremental small step forward, or back. Through it all, our key message was that we needed the sellers to take positive steps to keep the carousel in Minnesota: We needed them to accept our offer, to withdraw the carousel from the auction, to make good on their word that they really wanted the carousel to stay home.

Guernsey's auction house was doing its own share of public negotiations. Whenever a Twin Cities reporter called, Arlan Ettinger would raise the ante a bit. He said he had people from around the country showing interest in outbidding us but he couldn't name them. We were hearing from other sources that

Knott's Berry Farm might be interested, but we also heard that members of the National Carousel Association were telling them it would be bad publicity to whisk a carousel away from a community that was working to save it.

The city wanted some confirmation that the carousel was really worth the asking price, partly to ensure that if we defaulted on the loan, the city would be able to sell the carousel at or near the price we were paying. We assembled names of experts qualified to assess the value of carousel figures, and we passed these along to city staff. They selected Marge Swenson, editor of the magazine *Carousel Art Quarterly,* based in California. She visited the 20 horses stored in Pennsylvania en route to the auction, and she spent a day inspecting the figures that remained in Minnesota. On December 1, she met with city staff and said the carousel's worth was in the neighborhood of a million dollars. She announced this at a press conference as well. But the *Pioneer Press* was beginning to ask whether the carousel was really worth this much.

Two reporters, Aron Kahn and Brian Bonner, were working on separate stories about the rising prices being paid by collectors and about the value of this particular carousel. At the press conference they asked an embarrassing question: Did we and the city know that Marge Swenson had been paid by Guernsey's to write a piece about the value of carousel pieces for the auction catalog? Didn't this represent a conflict of interest? In fact, we had not known. Peter stayed cool. He said her estimate was in line with advice we had gotten from other experts and that we were negotiating for as low a price as possible. Privately, we wondered why she hadn't thought to tell the city, or us, about her relationship with Guernsey's.

Meanwhile Peter had contacted Bill Blinstrup with an oral offer of $1 million, payable in four equal installments over a period of nine months. Our goal was to limit the amount of interest we would have to pay on a loan, for which we were still shopping. The family rejected that offer November 29, saying they required a lump-sum payment. At the December 1 press conference where Marge Swenson was announcing her assessment of the carousel's value, Peter announced that he had asked the family to pull the carousel out of the auction. Bill Blinstrup had replied that the matter was out of the family's hands and only the auction house could take such an action. But at the press conference Peter and Marge Swenson both kept the pressure on, insisting that if the family made their wishes clear, Guernsey's would have to honor them. Then Peter uttered his most colorful sound bite ever. Since any competing bidders knew exactly how much money we had, he said, we were at a competitive disadvantage. They would know exactly what was necessary to outbid us. "Never," he said, "has a man gone so naked into an auction." Every reporter in the room quoted him.

While these negotiations were underway, Peter was contacting Saint Paul area banks to secure a loan. When he called First Bank (now US Bank), he was referred to Gary Woeltge, who headed the bank's work with non-profit organizations. Woeltge was an affable Saint Paul native who loved the state fair and had ridden the carousel often, and he was the first banker with whom Peter felt a personal connection. We knew that Our Fair Carousel was an unknown quantity and not the kind of startup that a bank would typically choose to support, but given how much public interest had been generated we hoped someone would welcome a chance to participate. Woeltge was that person, and happily for us he made the loan.

On Tuesday, December 6, as soon as we had agreed on the terms of the loan, Peter faxed a formal written offer to the Blinstrups and the auction house. We still hoped we could buy the carousel before the auction. We got no response, but on Wednesday Guernsey's co-owner Barbara Mintz told *Pioneer Press* reporter Brian Bonner that the carousel would remain in the auction. She said if the carousel were sold intact, it would be a great disappointment to people who were flying in from as far away as Hong Kong and Switzerland to bid on individual horses. She described the horses as "extraordinary animals," some of which could fetch $40,000 or more each. People coming to bid on them would be irate if not given the opportunity, she said.

Bonner called Peter for a response. We had been taking the high road, keeping a positive tone. Now time was running out, and Peter was blunt. He said he felt deceived by the family, who had consistently said they wanted the carousel to remain in Saint Paul. "I'm feeling shafted," he told Bonner. "Since other people know what my bid is, anybody who really wants it knows just how high they have to go to get it. What this means is despite everything Guernsey's told me, and Bill Blinstrup, and [Blinstrup attorney] Larry Harris, they aren't interested in where it goes. They're interested in getting the most money." Others were similarly harsh. City council member Bob Long told Bonner that the family's decision was "really a travesty." Marge Swenson, reached in California, said the family "wants to get top dollar, or they would have accepted the bid." She said the family and the auction house seemed focused on drawing wealthy collectors in hopes they would succumb to "auction fever."

After that story appeared in Thursday's morning paper, attorney Harris told both daily newspapers that the family had taken no action on our offer. He said they were still awaiting written proof of our loan, which they expected from First Bank later that day. He told *Star Tribune* reporter Anthony Lonetree that the family hadn't decided whether they would accept our offer, but that even if they wanted to, Guernsey's would also have to approve it. This time, Guernsey's Barbara Mintz said that if the auction house received proof of our loan the carousel would be sold intact. She was making no promises about withdrawing the carousel from the auction and selling directly to us. But she did say that the year before, Guernsey's had agreed to remove a carousel from an auction, selling it to the city of Saratoga, New York.

By Thursday afternoon it became clear that the rest of the negotiating would have to be done in New York. It was a good thing we had a pair of airline tickets and a hotel reservation. Friday morning we headed to First Bank headquarters in downtown Saint Paul to pick up a letter of credit for $1.3 million; this was the document that served as evidence of our loan. Peter tucked it into his breast pocket. We were all business, but a little nervous, as we headed to the gate for our flight. As we settled in at the waiting area, we noticed KARE TV's Allen Costantini, who had been reporting on the story. He and cameraman Tom Empe were on the same flight, also headed for the auction. Brian Bonner would be in New York as well. The *New York Times* Friday morning carried a column about Saturday's auctions at Sotheby's, Christie's, and Guernsey's; the longest segment was about our carousel and our efforts to save it. The woman writing the story had told us the auction might draw national attention, partly because it demonstrated a new high in the popularity of carousel figures and partly because there might be a dramatic story about a town saving its carousel.

Friday evening we checked into our hotel and then took a cab to the auction site, Pier 88 on the Hudson River. Just over 200 auction items were set out row upon row within the long room built in the 1930s as a passenger terminal for ocean-going ships. This would be our first opportunity to see "our" horses since getting so involved on their behalf. We walked slowly among them, rubbing their faces, appreciating the details of their saddles, blankets, decorations. We came upon the alligator horse, listed in the catalog at $35,000 to $40,000. Had we ever really looked closely at it at the fair? Had we noticed that the alligator held a fish in its mouth, and behind the cantle a turtle snapped at another fish? All of our horses had their charms. We were hopeful of rescuing them, but what if someone outbid us? This could be our last time to see these old friends. While Nancy was feeling waves of nostalgia and nervousness, Peter was keeping an eye out for Arlan Ettinger, who was busy greeting people as they arrived. Soon he welcomed us effusively and took time to show us some of the other prize pieces around the room. Two other carousels had been broken up for this auction (with, we were told, no community efforts to save them) and there were exceptional pieces from private collections. On another day, under other circumstances, this might have been fascinating. But now we needed to conclude a deal. Ettinger said the Blinstrup party had been at the pier and had left. We would have to wait until Saturday.

At some point Peter checked our phone messages at home. Brian Bonner had called Friday afternoon. He had been at the auction, talking to carousel fans about our horses. He found a number of "experts" who said we were about to pay far more than the carousel was worth. As a good reporter does, Bonner was offering us an opportunity to comment. Unfortunately, he filed the story while we were still en route to New York. In those days before everyone had cell phones, there had been no way to get our side of the story into the paper. Saturday morning Peter called one of our supporters, who read him the story. The headline, splashed across the top of page 1: "Experts at auction say price of carousel inflated."

The so-called experts seemed to have no expert credentials at all, and most of their comments were based on faulty assumptions. True, the most paid for a carousel at auction had been just under $700,000. But more had been paid in private sales, and no carousels for which records existed were the size and quality of this one. A woman said some of the horses had been repainted and were not in original paint, which we knew and which Marge Swenson had calculated into her estimate. A man said horses were badly damaged on their trip to New York and would be further damaged on their return. Having examined all the horses, we knew there were very few signs of fresh damage and what there was could easily be repaired. One man was sure it would take an extra $400,000 or more to restore the carousel before it could be ridden again. Someone said we should hire a woodcarver to create new figures; it could be done for $5,000 tops. Why pay all this money just to let kids ride on the horses? Peter was fuming as he listened to the story over the phone. The comments were unfounded, and the overall impression could make our fund-raising much more difficult. But we had to forget about the story and focus on the problem at hand.

Peter had told Larry Harris where we were staying, and Harris called early Saturday morning to say he had a room in the same hotel. And that's where they hammered out a purchase agreement. In a hand-written two-page document they specified the purchase price along with details such as when the closing would take place, who would pay for the horses to be returned to Minnesota, and who would pay for insurance until the closing. Harris wrote each paragraph on a yellow lined legal pad, and Peter hurried to fax a copy to our *pro bono* attorney Jerry Paquin, standing by at his Minneapolis office. Peter had to resend the fax a couple of times before it went through, but by a little after 10 a.m. the agreement was approved by Our Fair Carousel and the Blinstrup family attorney. Now it just needed Arlan Ettinger's signature.

The auction was scheduled to begin at 1 p.m. At about 10:30, we let Allen Costantini and Tom Empe know we were leaving soon for the auction. They had stayed at the same hotel, and they wanted to get to the auction when we did. The morning was sunny but bitterly cold and windy, and there were no cabs in sight. The four of us walked a block or two to the Plaza Hotel, where there would be a cab line. Cabs were much in demand and we were all freezing as we made a quick decision to share one, squeezing Tom's camera equipment in among us for the five-minute trip.

As our cab neared the pier, we saw a small group of demonstrators holding signs and shouting. We recognized Fred Fried, whose book celebrating the art of the carousel, published 20 years earlier, had fueled much of the current popular interest. Fried had been dismayed that appreciation for carousel figures eventually led to the breakup of working rides for the benefit of collectors. He had made his views known in interviews about our efforts, and he had said he would protest if Guernsey's didn't release the carousel to us before the auction. Riding by, Nancy found herself smiling at the group and wanting to say, "Hey, we're the good guys." That opportunity came later, when the demonstrators came into the pier to warm up. We hurried over to Fred Fried and introduced ourselves. "You're our hero," Nancy said. "On the contrary," he replied, "You are my heroes."

By the time we arrived, Guernsey's was beginning to move some of the displayed items aside in order to set out chairs and an auction platform. Arlan Ettinger kept himself busy greeting people and occasionally ducking into a small makeshift office space behind the platform. The crowd was growing, and people were beginning to claim good seats. Peter quickly threw our coats on a pair of folding chairs in the front row, very near the spot where Ettinger would conduct the auction. We could see that a couple of cloth coats would not be enough to secure the seats in this mostly wealthy, mostly privileged crowd, so Nancy sat down to safeguard our spot. When someone put out a new row of chairs, creating a new front row, she grabbed the coats and moved up. She was not going to be elbowed aside. At the same time, she knew people were talking about the group that was here to save Minnesota's carousel, and she tried not to draw attention to herself or Peter before the deal was done. When people on either side of her made small talk, she responded with more small talk. But it was hard to stay calm.

Time was ticking away. Larry Harris had brought the purchase agreement to Ettinger, but Ettinger wasn't signing. He said someone was prepared to bid against us, and they could pay as much as $1.3 million. Guernsey's, which got 10 percent of the auction price from the seller and 10 percent from the buyer, would be giving up income if it pulled the carousel from the auction. He said we should assume someone would pay $150,000 more than we bid; the auction house's share would then go up by $30,000. He wanted Our Fair Carousel and the Blinstrups to jointly pay him that much extra. Peter said we didn't have that much. He ran through the numbers. Our loan was $1.3 million. The purchase price and Guernsey's 10 percent totaled $1.1 million. We had to pay interest on the loan as well as storage and insurance for the horses. "I've been up-front about this all along," he said. "You can't squeeze blood from a stone." He had been standing in a tight cluster with Bill Blinstrup, Larry Harris, and Arlan Ettinger at the side of the room, silhouetted against the window. Now he sat down next to Nancy and let the others continue to negotiate.

Just moments after 1 p.m. Ettinger mounted the platform and began the auction. He sold a handful of small items that had not been included in the catalog. We still had no agreement. The first of our horses was auction item six. If the agreement wasn't signed by the time that horse sold, the old state fair carousel was gone forever. While the first item from the catalog itself was being placed on the platform, Ettinger left his spot to rejoin Blinstrup and Harris on the sidelines. Peter hurried over. Bill Blinstrup told Ettinger he would pay Ettinger's new demand and cover whatever part of OFC's share we couldn't cover. Peter said we could pay $7,500. The deal was done. New figures were hastily inserted into the document, Ettinger signed it, and there was a handshake. Few people in the room noticed. One who did was KARE's Tom Empe, who realized what was happening just in time to catch the moment on videotape. Nancy, too, had seen the handshake. She didn't ask out loud; instead she gave Peter a slightly raised eyebrow. He answered with a subtle nod. Together we waited as the next few auction pieces slowly, slowly, were sold.

Then it was time for the first horse from our carousel. Instead of the one shown in the catalog, Ettinger brought up the pinto pony, a favorite of riders, distinctive for its decorations, and featured on the cover of the auction catalog. A murmur began to spread through the room. Ettinger took in the moment, and then made his announcement. When they tell the story of this carousel, he said, they will talk about a community that loved it and about people who worked together to save it. Ettinger introduced Bill Blinstrup and told the crowd that Guernsey's and Blinstrup had decided not to take any other bids in order to keep the carousel in Minnesota. Then he introduced Peter, who walked over and shook hands, the new owner sealing the deal with the former owner.

As Peter remembers it, Ettinger's announcement brought a few boos. Perhaps they were from people who had come to bid on the horses individually. Or perhaps they were from people who thought Arlan Ettinger gave himself and Bill Blinstrup too much credit for keeping the carousel in Minnesota. We'll never know. Nancy only heard cheers and applause, and congratulations from people seated around us. News photographers materialized with still and video cameras. We made our way to the back of the hall where we answered questions for Brian Bonner and Allen Costantini as well as for the *New York Times*, CNN, a stringer for the *Star*

Tribune, and other media. We said we were happy. We said we did this because carousels are an American art form and fun to ride. We said we were doing this for our future grandchildren. We said we still had more than a million dollars to raise but we were confident it would happen. The television people asked us to walk over and pose with one of the horses we had just saved. We stood on each side of the horse, looked across at one another...and kissed. It was a spontaneous celebration of what we had just accomplished together. Apparently it was also the ultimate way to embarrass a 12-year-old daughter. Today we all laugh about her response. "Ugh, you guys kissed on national television. How could you do that *to me*?"

In Chicago that Saturday afternoon, Peter's friend Marie, with whom we had visited months earlier on our cross-country carousel-visiting trip, happened to be watching CNN. Promoting their evening news, CNN said they had a story about high prices paid at a New York carousel auction. "Hey, we'll have to watch that so we can tell Peter and Nancy about it," she said to her husband. A few minutes later the story was on the air. "Oh my gosh, it *is* Peter and Nancy!"

Back home after a very intense couple of days, we found that the television news story by Allen Costantini and Tom Empe was a wonderful way to relive an incredible experience. We could watch it without feeling all the nervousness of the day, secure in the knowledge that the auction story had a happy ending. We noticed the wealthy and well-dressed people all around us, whom we had mostly blocked out in order to focus on the task at hand. Watching it, we sometimes had the same reaction as our friend Marie. "Oh my gosh, it *is* Peter and Nancy!"

The purchase became official at a closing ceremony at First Bank on December 22. We had hoped to generate a lot of media coverage so we could use the occasion to remind people that there was much fund-raising ahead. The usual media outlets had said they would be there, but at the appointed hour few showed up. A plane bound for the United States had been downed over Lockerbie, Scotland, the previous day and media people were busy pursuing local angles. It was a somber time and a reminder that the carousel would not always be at the center of attention.

In the end, we paid $1.132 million to buy the carousel. Guernsey's had sold the rest of the items for $2.9 million, the highest total for a carousel sale. A 1908 horse with a flying gold mane, carved by Marcus Charles Illions, sold for $101,750, a record for a single carousel figure. Three months later a carousel rooster sold for $148,000, and overall prices continued to rise. But to us, the important story was not the record amounts being paid for carousels and their figures. The important fact was this: five or six operating carousels were being lost *every year*. At the time, we couldn't find a single grass-roots group that had managed to save one. We were fighting against the tide to save a beautiful and well-loved piece of Americana, and to keep it in our community where people loved it.

We needed to raise more than a million dollars, but we had two secret weapons for the continuing struggle. One, which a few people were beginning to discover, was that we had become thoroughly committed and determined to succeed in saving the carousel. We were willing to take on any challenge, and work all night whenever necessary. The other, which we had revealed to no one, would shape the carousel's story as much as Austin McFadden and David Lightfoot had done decades earlier.

4

The Mystery Donor

On a Saturday afternoon in December 1988, a week before the Guernsey's auction, we got a phone call from a man whose generosity would give new life to an otherwise doomed carousel. Saint Paul businessman Gerard L. Cafesjian, or Jerry, had fallen in love with carousels in New York and New Jersey as a young boy. Moving to Minnesota as an adult, he would visit the state fair and stop to watch — and sometimes ride — the beautiful PTC carousel at Commonwealth and Underwood. Now, learning that it was to be sold, he stepped forward with an extraordinarily generous donation that helped save it. With more gifts he would help fund both its restoration and its new home. That's why a carousel known variously as PTC 33, the state fair carousel, and "World's Largest Merry-Go-Round" entered its new life as Cafesjian's Carousel.

Jerry Cafesjian's parents were Armenian immigrants whose families were among more than a million Armenians killed by the Ottoman Empire between 1915 and 1923. The couple settled in Brooklyn, New York, where they were determined to endow their children with a sense that life could be happy in spite of hardship. Jerry's father lost his diner during the Great Depression. On the day of the foreclosure he stopped on the way home to buy cake and chocolates for the family, Jerry recalled. "He wanted us to know we would be okay."

While Jerry's father worked through hot New York summers, the rest of the family escaped the heat at the Jersey shore. Young Jerry, with his mother and sister, stayed in a boardinghouse near the beautiful Asbury Park carousel. As he fell asleep each night, the lights of the carousel danced across the ceiling of his room and the band organ music was a lively lullaby. He never forgot that experience and how happy it made him. His family also rode carousels at Coney Island, and when he was old enough he ventured there alone, boarding the subway near his home in Brooklyn and riding to the last stop.

Serving in the Navy during World War II, Jerry met a nurse named Cleo Thomas; they married soon after the war. After earning degrees in economics and law he became a legal editor at the New York office of West Publishing Company, producer of law reference books. His talents caught the attention of company managers, who moved him to the home office in Saint Paul. By the end of his career he was executive vice president, heading up sales, marketing, customer service, and other fields. He was also a major shareholder in the privately owned company.

When we met Jerry he owned one carousel horse and had two working miniature carousels on display in his office. But his passion for art was much more far-reaching. He and Cleo filled their home — and eventually a second home and more than one museum — with sculpture, colorful art glass, and charmingly whimsical pieces. The art he collected tended to emphasize form, color, light, and delight, the same elements he had come to love while watching and riding carousels. (Years later he built an eclectic collection of carousel figures and twice put some of them on public display in Minneapolis during the winter holidays.)

As soon as it became clear that we, not the city, would be negotiating to buy the carousel, Jerry sent us a check for $100. We hadn't

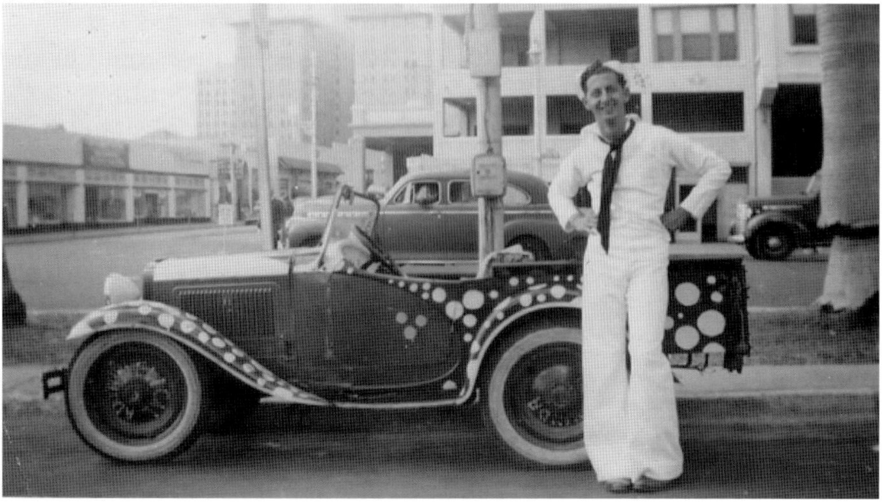

Young sailor on leave. Jerry Cafesjian's taste in art always ran toward the whimsical, like this polka-dot car. We like to think he was on his way to pick up his girlfriend, nurse Cleo Thomas, to take her to Coney Island for a carousel ride. *By permission of the Estate of Gerard L. Cafesjian*

received many checks of that size so we decided to check him out. His name appeared on membership lists of both the National Carousel Association and the American Carousel Society, and because he used his business address on his correspondence we saw that he was a downtown businessman—just the sort of person we needed for the Our Fair Carousel board. Peter quickly called to invite him to serve, and he agreed.

On the day Jerry called to discuss a gift, he asked Peter, "Assuming you're successful in buying the carousel, what do you plan to do with it?" Peter said we intended to operate it for the public somewhere in Saint Paul. He told Jerry the original paint was in good condition under the varnish and we planned to restore it. "You're not going to let a bunch of kids in grimy jeans and scratchy belt buckles ride it, are you?" Jerry asked. Peter replied, "A carousel is meant to be ridden. If we don't preserve it as a working carousel we might as well let the collectors have it."

"That's the right answer," Jerry said.

He told Peter he had planned to have a carousel made. Now he was thinking it might be better to help save this carousel. "What would it cost to put my name on it?" Jerry asked. He explained that his immediate family was the last with the name Cafesjian. With no male grandchildren to carry the name forward, he was looking for other ways to keep it alive. Peter asked him to hold on for a minute. He covered the mouthpiece and repeated the question to Nancy. Drawing on what she had learned from fundraising colleagues at work, she said, "A naming gift is at least half the cost of the project." Peter uncovered the mouthpiece. "Six hundred thousand dollars."

"Done," said Jerry.

Jerry Cafesjian was unusual among carousel benefactors. He could have simply purchased an intact carousel and found a place to operate it, or he could have taken all the best figures and displayed them at home or in a museum. Instead, he made a gift to save a carousel he knew was well loved in its home community. He later told reporter Brian Bonner that when he paused to watch the carousel at the state fair, he enjoyed hearing and *feeling* the music, watching the lights and painted horses, and especially watching the faces of the riders. When he learned it was at risk, he said, he realized "it was too good to break up and toss away."

Jerry participated actively on the OFC board and brought along business associates who provided legal and financial expertise. He contributed funds to help restore the horses and chariots, to purchase and restore a band organ, and eventually to build a new pavilion to house the carousel in Como Park. By the time of his death in September 2013, he had doubled his initial gift for a total of $1.2 million. He visited the carousel every summer, often bringing a few out-of-town associates to experience it. Sometimes he followed up with a letter to the volunteers, telling them how much he appreciated the care they showed for the horses and riders.

When Jerry contacted us in 1988, he was a very private man who had kept a low profile. We decided to wait several months before announcing Jerry's gift, and then we announced it as a pledge from an anonymous donor. This kept his name out of the media, and it also protected his money. If we failed to raise enough to repay Our Fair Carousel's bank loan, the agreement we had signed

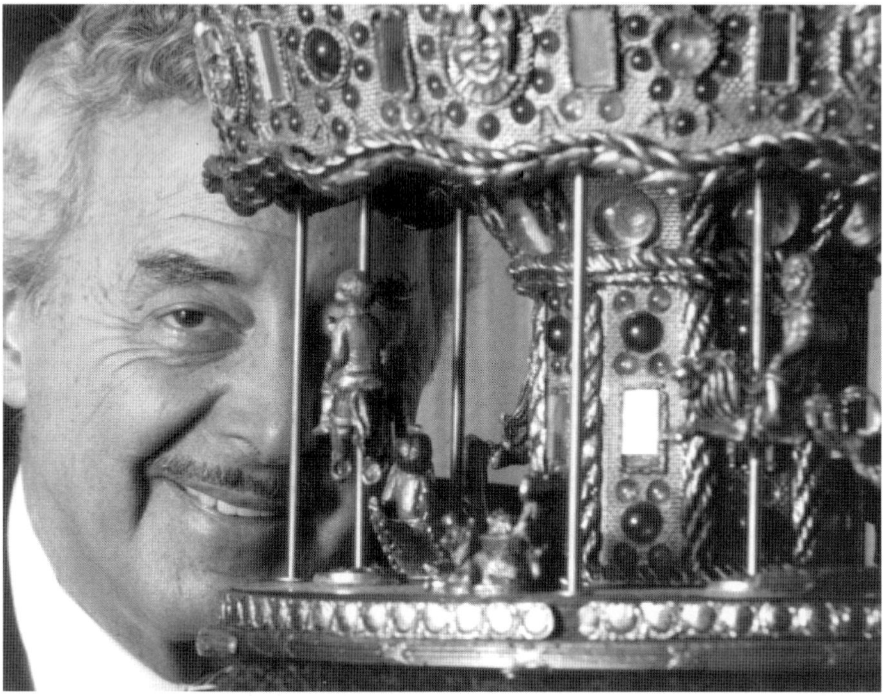

A very private man, Jerry Cafesjian agreed to give two newspaper interviews when we announced his identity as the carousel's mystery donor. This is one of two small carousels he kept in his office. *Photo by Joe Oden, Saint Paul Pioneer Press*

said the city could take over the carousel *and* the donations we had raised. By pledging funds but not transferring them, Jerry would not be at risk. The pledge buoyed our spirits as we approached the auction, but we told only one person. We met with Mayor Latimer to tell him an anonymous donor was pledging $600,000 and in return wanted the carousel named for him. Latimer didn't miss a beat. "Bye-bye, Joe," he said, referring to KARE-11 president Franzgrote. Jerry, too, kept the secret; for more than a year he did not mention his gift to friends, or even his children.

When the Our Fair Carousel board of directors met for the first time in early March 1989, members were delighted to learn of the "mystery donor" pledge. They speculated on his identity, unaware that he was seated uncomfortably among them at the table. Jerry said later that he'd wished he could disappear.

Two days after that board meeting, reporters were speculating, too. We held a news conference to announce that the carousel was going to Town Square Park and to announce the anonymous $600,000 pledge. When Peter told reporters that the donor was a Minnesota man whose name was not a household word they began a game of 20 questions, tossing out prominent names of long-time Minnesota business leaders. Dayton? No. Pillsbury? No. Ordway? No. Pohlad? No. Eventually they ran out of guesses. "When we complete the fund-raising and the gift is given, we will reveal his name," Peter promised.

When that time came, in March 1990, we had a second anonymous gift to announce. A University of Minnesota journalism graduate student named Diane Bush had called to say she planned to adopt a pony for $10,000, using funds she had recently inherited from her parents. Peter invited her to the house to look at photos so she could select a horse. She arrived at lunch time, so he cooked up an omelet and they sat at the kitchen table chatting about the project, which had begun right at that table. By the end of lunch, Diane had changed her pledge from $10,000 to $75,000, adopting four horses in honor of family members. Afterward, Peter often joked that it must have been the best omelet he'd ever made.

Diane's studies emphasized photography and other visual arts. She was captivated by carousel figures while living on the West Coast, and as an undergraduate she had researched the art of carousels for a college paper. "I've been looking for a way to share my good fortune with others," she told *Pioneer Press* reporter Thomas Collins. "My money can't save the world but it can help save this carousel."

A reporter once asked Jerry Cafesjian why he chose to direct his money toward the carousel instead of, say, fighting hunger or disease. In fact, it was never an either-or situation. Jerry supported other causes, as do most of our donors and volunteers. Philanthropy became a major focus beginning in 1996 when West Publishing Company was sold and Jerry, as a major owner, received a significant amount of money.

He decided that life had brought him a unique opportunity to help rebuild his ancestral nation of Armenia. After decades of being ruled by other countries including the Soviet Union, Armenia had declared its independence in 1991, but people were poor and the infrastructure was in ruins. Jerry contributed $128 million to projects including a renewable energy company, two television stations, and the rebuilding of a massive and crumbling Soviet structure in downtown Yerevan that is now a gathering place and home to the Cafesjian Center for the Arts. It was the president of Armenia who in 2013 announced Jerry's death to the world.

Jerry knew first-hand the happiness a carousel ride can bring to children and adults alike. He told the *Star Tribune's* Joe Kimball, "I saw this as a special way that I could offer a measure of happiness to children of all ages and our community as a whole." Twenty-five years later, Cafesjian's Carousel continues to delight, and children of all ages are grateful.

5
Come Join the Carnival

In its first 74 years at the Minnesota State Fair, the carousel gave hundreds of thousands of riders a chance to imagine they were princesses, knights, cowboys, adventurers. In 1989 the carousel provided one lucky group a different kind of fantasy. Dozens of volunteers got the chance to pretend they had run away to join the carnival. For three hours at a time — the duration of a single volunteer shift — people left behind whatever else they did in life to operate a very large amusement ride. It was hard work in a dusty, noisy, crowded, and often hot building. But many who worked one shift quickly signed up for more, and some came back every day. For 74 years the carousel had been staffed mostly by a paid mechanic or a few members of an owner's family. Now volunteers were both necessary and welcome, and we would learn together how to do the job.

We had no owner's manual, and some of our learning was done through trial and error. The carousel was in pieces; all 68 horses and the hardware to support them had to be placed back on the carousel platform. We expected a challenge, but what we got was far more difficult than we imagined.

Over the years, the carousel has brought together people with just the right skills, just when they are needed. Arthur Curtze was one of those people. In our first few days of setting up Our Fair Carousel and seeking information and advice, someone passed along the name of Art Curtze of State College, Pennsylvania, a man dedicated to saving carousels, knowledgeable about their value, and well connected within the carousel world. He took a keen interest, calling Peter nearly every night in those early weeks, bringing up all kinds of things we should know about buying and operating a ride. Art had a great deal of experience with the mechanics of Philadelphia Toboggan Company machines, and people told us his work was exacting and reliable. He agreed to serve on the OFC board and to come to Minnesota for a week to help get the carousel operational. He would arrive the Friday before the fair and stay until Thursday, the opening day. He would help us get the horses back on the machine, and he would supervise the mechanical work of checking, cleaning, lubricating, and adjusting the working parts until the ride ran smoothly. He would also train a mechanic who would work the duration of the fair.

We found a local mechanic named Bill Drager who had worked on a PTC machine that operated on the midway some years before. By the time we met him he was 71 and could no longer climb to the upper structure where much of the work needed to be done. For that he brought his 16-year-old grandson, Art Drager, as strong and nimble a climber as you'd ever want to meet. Arthur Curtze confirmed that young Art was a good mechanic, well trained by his grandfather. By the end of the first day, Bill had bowed out and we had hired Art in his place.

We showed up at the carousel building the Saturday before the fair expecting to get all the horses on the platform by Sunday. Without the horses, the building seemed enormous and gaping. And it chirped. That is, at least half of the dozen-or-so smoke detectors chirped. We made a mental note to change the batteries and got down to business. All morning, more than a dozen people cleaned the platform and motor house, scrubbing away grease spots and remnants of prior years' traffic. At noon trucks brought the horses from storage, and a group of former high school wrestlers carried them in and stacked them against the walls. Under Arthur Curtze's direction, the wrestlers and other strong volunteers began to assemble the horses and install them on the platform. As they did, the cleaning continued. Dodie Paul and other artists washed the horses with Murphy's Oil Soap. Board member Muriel Poehler used her carpentry skills to repair a broken piece of the center motor housing while her young twin daughters polished brass. Several people who regularly worked at the fair, like Sandy Greeley who sold French fries and Bob Crump who helped his wife Pat manage the fair's art exhibit, did whatever was needed.

Sandy had recruited the wrestlers, including her son. They and the others working on the horses had the day's big challenge. Their task was to place a brass sleeve around a steel rod, slide it through a horse, and add a metal step. Then we would hang the horse from an overhead crank shaft and connect it to the platform with a telescoping support. But there was a problem that even Arthur Curtze had never encountered: It was nearly impossible to force the collar of the step onto the steel rod. The step looked like it was made to slide into place, but every collar was too tight. We had to pound each one forcefully, bracing it with a two-by-four and hitting that with a large mallet, inching the step into position. The two-by-fours split from the pounding and even the strongest wrestlers soon found their shoulders aching. (Only years later did we solve this problem when two volunteers invented a tool that spread the step apart just enough that we could slide it onto the pole.)

In addition, when the horses had been hastily taken off the carousel in November, the hardware was treated as if it would never be used again. Brass sleeves were bent and scraped and tossed on a pile. "We're having a terrible time," Bill Drager told *Star Tribune* reporter Conrad deFiebre. "It looks like they abused it in their hurry to take it apart."

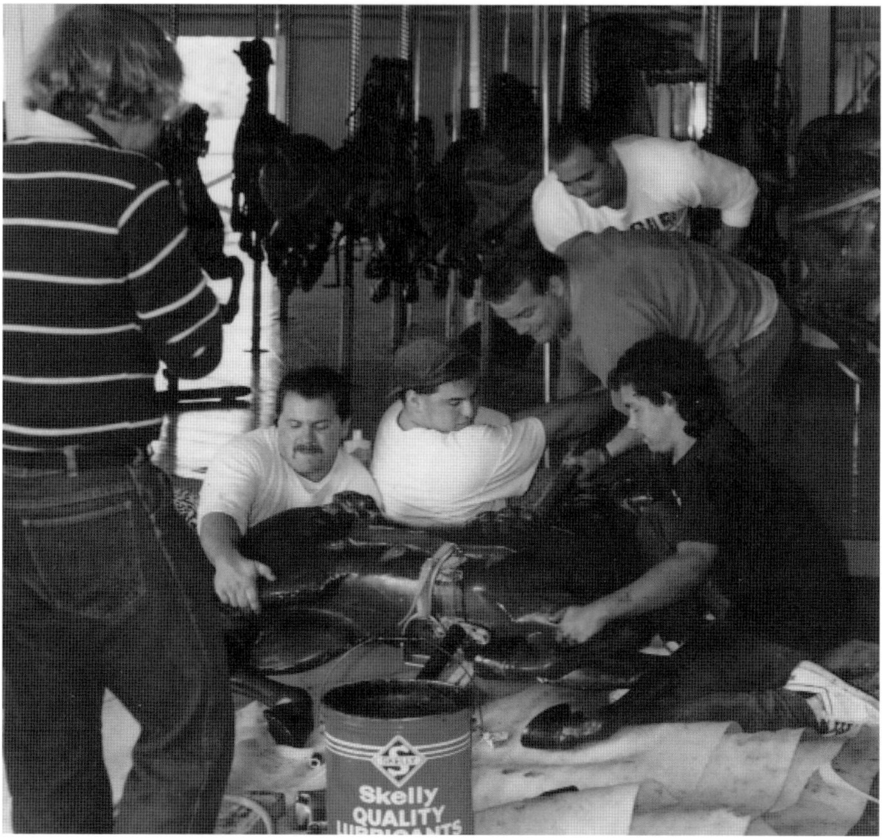

Art Drager, in dark shirt, and volunteers wrestle the pole into a horse as news photographers capture their struggle.

By the end of Saturday, about half the horses were on the ride. Not all the volunteers could return Sunday, but some returned with an extra friend or two. So the work proceeded. We knew enough to put the smallest horses on the innermost row, the biggest on the outer row, and the intermediate ones in rows two and three. But Sunday night, with most of the horses in place and workers ready to hang the last few, we made a wrenching discovery: The remaining steel poles were too long. In disbelief, Peter and Arthur Curtze realized that the poles needed to be different lengths for different rows. The platform is slightly tilted toward the inside, so poles on the outer row must be an inch or two shorter than those on the inner row. At the end of two very long days, we would have to take many of the horses back off and find the sixteen shortest poles. We would have to wrestle those poles free to use them on the outer row and reassemble the smaller horses with the longer poles.

Peter's confidence has buoyed us through difficult moments before and since, but that night he was distraught. We had lost valuable time and wasted the efforts of hard-working volunteers. Only a few could return on Monday, and there was much to be done before the fair started Thursday. *Too* much, Peter thought. Even if we got the horses on, what other problems awaited us? When he finally got home at midnight, he felt defeated. "We aren't going to get it done," he said. It was our darkest night in the history of the project, before or since.

We didn't give up, of course. More important than the money we needed to earn was our credibility. Who would believe in Our Fair Carousel if we couldn't even get the machine running on time? So early Monday morning Peter, Arthur Curtze, Art Drager, and a handful of determined and generous volunteers were back at the carousel building. The work was hard and we had not quite enough people, but we kept at it for two more days. With the 68 horses and both chariots on board at last, Curtze and Drager began to adjust the overhead gears so each horse would run smoothly. They also positioned each row so the horses would rise and fall in waves as the machine turned. It's a fine point but it makes a carousel more pleasing to watch.

After midnight, Curtze had the carousel running continuously to let the newly adjusted and lubricated parts settle in together. Peter watched the horses run and leap, and he listened to the gentle creaking of the gears. This time when he came home he said quietly, "The horses are happy. The carousel was turning, they were going up and down, and they told me they are happy." Says Nancy, "Peter was exhausted and I thought he was delirious. But the horses might indeed have been happy. They were together again, and they were going to the fair!"

By the time he had finished his work, Arthur Curtze said the carousel was one of the smoothest-running he had ever encountered. He went home on the first day of the fair as planned, but he remained on the OFC board until 2013, returning twice a year to maintain the mechanical quality of the ride. By the time he retired from the board he was calling it the smoothest-running carousel in the country. It's a standard we try to uphold.

While this work was going on, volunteers from the Guthrie Theatre decorated the carousel with ribbons that waved in the breeze and set up theatrical lights to give the horses a special glow. We set up a photo display to tell our story and brought in folding tables from which we would sell merchandise. We put tickets in the machine and change in the cash drawer and we scheduled volunteers to operate the carousel in three-hour shifts. The schedule wasn't full, but we hoped it would fill in as the fair went on.

On Thursday morning, the first day of the fair, we were mopping up random grease spots, setting out merchandise, and briefing volunteers on their roles when media people began to arrive. We were due to open at 9 a.m.; by 8:45 the building was filling with reporters, camera people, and their equipment preparing to capture the opening moments of what we called the carousel's "75th and final season" at the fair. Even with theatrical lights the building was dim, so when television people asked to plug in their lights, we accommodated them.

We knew that the key to attracting riders early in the day was to have the carousel spinning and music playing even before you open the doors. So at exactly 9 a.m., with the doors still closed, Peter rang the carousel's warning bell and pushed the start button. The machine groaned a bit as it gathered strength to begin turning...and it stopped. The building plunged into darkness. There was a moment of shocked silence until Peter shouted, "Unplug the TV lights; we need the power for the carousel." He reset the circuit breakers and on the second try the carousel started up smoothly. We threw open the big garage doors across the front of the building, letting in plenty of daylight for the cameras. The music played, the ticket booth opened, people lined up with dollars in hand, and we were in business.

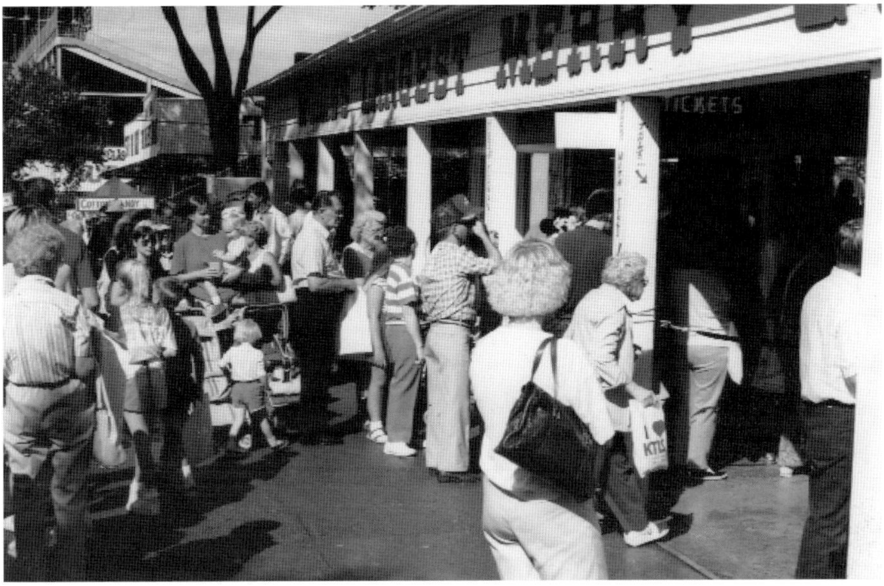

People were eager to ride the carousel during its last run at the fair-and, if we failed to raise enough money, possibly its last run anywhere.

Any time we had ridden the carousel in the past, you simply walked up and bought your tickets, waited around the edge for it to stop, and climbed on. Because we expected crowds, we had set up ropes around the carousel, with an entry on the left and an exit on the right. It took less than an hour to realize that we had a crowd control problem. We tried to get people to line up near the entry point. But the line quickly became a crowd and then a bottleneck. If you moved to let someone pass, you risked losing your place. People inside had trouble wading through the crowd to get out.

On day two, we brought in stanchions to manage the line, but the real problem was too many people for the size of the building. Then Sally Brewer, one of our ticket sellers, had a brilliant idea. Instead of selling tickets as fast as possible, she could slow down her pace and sell just enough for the next ride. We figured out how long the line inside needed to be. When it got that long, she paused. As soon as the line began moving again, she resumed selling. It worked. The line waiting to buy tickets extended a little farther down the block, but once people got in, they only waited a few minutes, and the bottleneck was gone. We felt like geniuses.

In addition to mechanic Art Drager, we had a crew of four volunteers on the ride at all times. Today's volunteers get hours of training in a detailed set of safety procedures based on years of experience. At the 1989 fair, we greeted a new set of volunteers every three hours, handed them a t-shirt, and told them to keep people — and horses — safe. There were already signs that said "Do not step on horses' legs." We learned to watch for a few other things. Don't hang purses or shopping bags from horses' ears. Don't place coolers beneath horses' legs. Don't walk around while the platform is moving.

If volunteers were lucky, they got to work a ride or two with the previous shift, who would share whatever pointers they could. This also allowed the newcomers to practice taking a few steps while the carousel was in motion. Centrifugal force pushes your body outward when you walk forward on a moving platform, and centripetal force pulls you toward the center when you walk back against the motion of the machine. Today's volunteers practice until they are comfortable with these forces so they can move easily to a rider who needs assistance. Practice time was a luxury we didn't have in 1989, but those of us who worked on the ride a lot began to get the hang of it, and as we gained confidence some of us developed a little carnival swagger.

Fortunately for everyone, riders were in good moods and on good behavior. There were no injuries, and only one horse suffered a broken leg. The knee had clearly been broken before, as had many on the carousel. Bob Crump, who had been stopping in every day, saw us gathered around the leg. "No problem," he said, and he left to fetch glue and a brace. While he fixed the break, we talked about the fact that as long as there have been carousels, horses' broken legs have been patched on the run.

By day four we came up with a way to minimize the time it took to get people on and off the carousel. At the end of a ride, two volunteers would start by the entry gate and "sweep" the people getting off, gently moving them toward the exit. When those

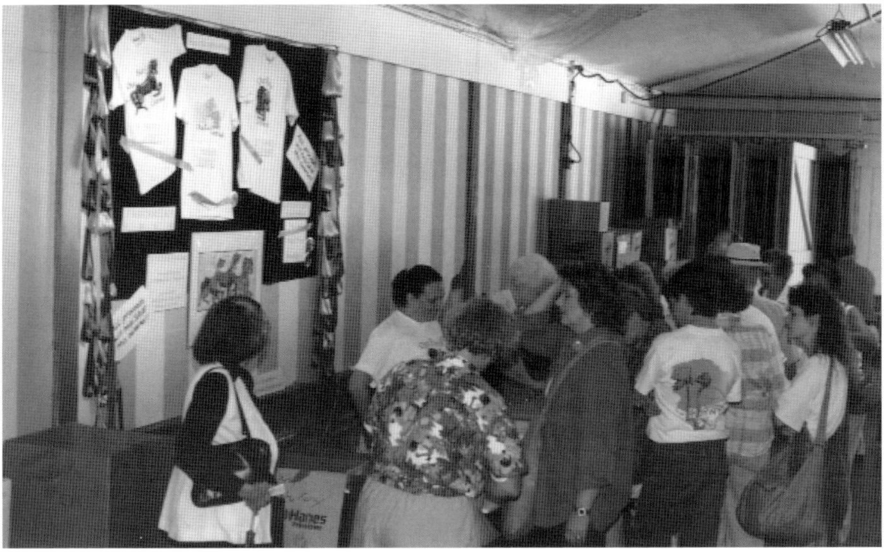

Volunteers at the makeshift gift booth were surrounded by people eager to take home a remembrance of the carousel's final year at the fair.

volunteers reached the halfway mark, others opened the entrance gate and let people begin to board. Once all the previous riders were out, the volunteers helped everyone get settled quickly. The ride itself was on a timer; everyone got their full two minutes. But we took pride in being able to load and unload quickly, and at our best we could start a new ride every six minutes. (We now give a longer four-minute ride, and operate at a more leisurely pace—a new ride every 12 minutes.)

Managing our lines and achieving quick turnarounds on the ride made a big difference. On that first day of milling crowds and totally inexperienced volunteers (including ourselves), we managed 7,400 riders. We had two days of 7,900 riders. But on our best nine days we gave 8,600 to 9,800 rides each day, and that's how we managed to accommodate 107,000 in 12 days — the most rides the carousel ever gave in one season at the fair.

Exiting the carousel, people walked right toward our sales area: t-shirts and posters $10, buttons $1. On the first morning, three volunteers stood ready. When the first ride ended they were inundated, and two more jumped in to help. We had thought one person could operate the cash register, but sales were too brisk and one cashier couldn't keep up. Besides, change-making was easy with our round-number prices, so each volunteer could do it. The cash drawer overflowed and so did the cigar boxes we added later, and still people came, grabbing shirts and buttons and thrusting money at volunteers.

At one point on that first day, a teenage volunteer stopped Peter, who was hurrying past. "I need to give you something," she said urgently. His hands were full of cash from the ticket booth so he motioned her toward the office, where she reached into her pockets and fished out wads of crumpled bills. We quickly made it a top priority to round up the cash early and often.

A combination safe in the office took too long to open — an annoyance when you had to do it a dozen times a day. Besides, if you ran into the office with your hands full of cash you had to drop it somewhere while you fiddled with the dial. Invariably somebody would walk in just then. So we got into the habit of wrapping a couple of rubber bands around a wad of bills and tossing the whole thing out of sight atop a high steel cabinet. At the end of the day Peter would climb onto a step stool and drop all the bundles of money to the desk, where he counted it until well past midnight. It went into the safe overnight, and he delivered it to the State Fair office at 7 a.m.

We had ordered our products conservatively, having no idea how much people would buy. But those who came to ride knew this was the carousel's last year at the fair. They wanted mementos, they wanted to help save it, and they bought everything in sight. By the second day we were reordering shirts and buttons; volunteers came early to meet the truck at the main gate and rush the boxes down the street before we opened.

For 12 days, rain or shine, people came to enjoy the ride and buy products. They read the newspaper articles we had on display, asked questions, wished us good luck. And they thanked us. People especially recognized Peter from his many media appearances, and all day long at the carousel and around the grounds they stopped him to say thanks. Twin Cities media, who move their news operations to the fair every day, continued to feature the carousel, and several outstate reporters came to do stories. We were interviewed by a writer for the *Christian Science Monitor* who made our project the focus of a lengthy story about the rising value of carousels; the story later was repeated in publications around the world, including the *Saudi Gazette* and a paper in Reykjavik, Iceland. People from concessions that neighbored the carousel stopped in to say how much they would miss it. Men who had worked for previous owners came by to share bits of useful information.

On Labor Day, the last day of the fair, we closed with a Volunteer Ride. We packed at least 80 people on the machine and it groaned mightily as it got up to speed. Emotions ran high. We were elated, celebrating our successful run. At the same time, if we failed to pay off the loan, this could indeed be the last ride ever. Most of us were smiling broadly even as tears streamed down our cheeks.

By the end of the fair, we had taken in $107,000 in ride fares, $160,000 in sales, and $4,600 in donations dropped into a barrel. We were exhausted from long hours and lack of sleep, but exhilarated as well. We had come to know the carousel, the feel of its power, the rhythm of a ride cycle, the teamwork of an effective crew. Volunteers couldn't wait to take the carousel apart, restore the mechanism, and get it operating in Town Square. By October we had disassembled the entire carousel, which had not been apart since 1939, carefully marked every piece, and photographed every step so we'd know how to put it together again. It all went into storage and we got back to fund-raising.

6
The Day the Clown Cried

The decade of the 1990s was a remarkable one in the life of Minnesota's most famous antique carousel. Having left its 75-year home, the ride known to the media as "the old state fair carousel" got a new name and moved to an indoor urban park where it was surrounded by green plants and glass ceilings. Volunteers spent the entire decade restoring the carousel's original beauty and they restored a band organ to make the rider's experience complete. When the downtown location proved to be only a transitional home, Cafesjian's Carousel began a journey to Saint Paul's Como Park — a mile east of its original location — where it quietly opened for a few days in fall 1999. It was a satisfying way to close the decade.

For Our Fair Carousel and its board, the decade was full of highs and lows and running in circles — like a carousel ride, but less fun. To begin with, we entered 1990 with unfinished business. We had set out to raise $1.3 million by the end of 1989. We — Peter and Nancy — had spent a year visiting prospective donors and writing to corporate and family foundations, making the case for the

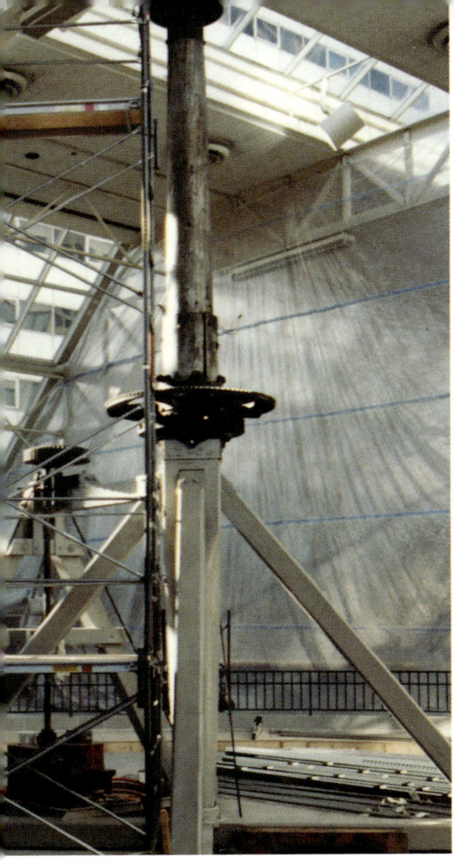

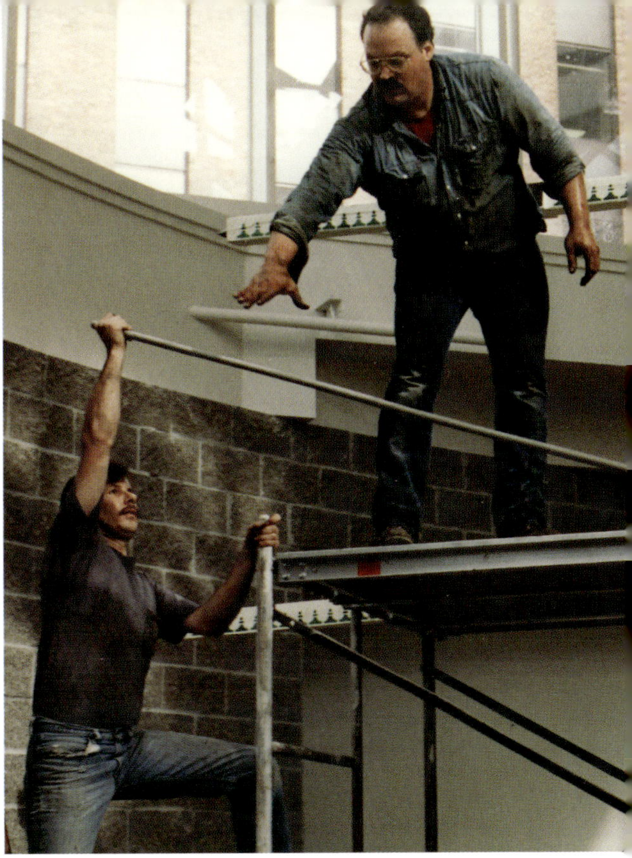

The 25-foot center pole rises into position at Town Square Park in fall 1990. Working on a scaffold, volunteer Keith Lowinski hands to millwright Mike Drimmel one of the rods from which the carousel will be suspended. Lower left, millwrights adjust the central bevel gear; we later discovered it required new shims to compensate for a flawed center pole. Right, hanging and wiring newly painted rounding boards.

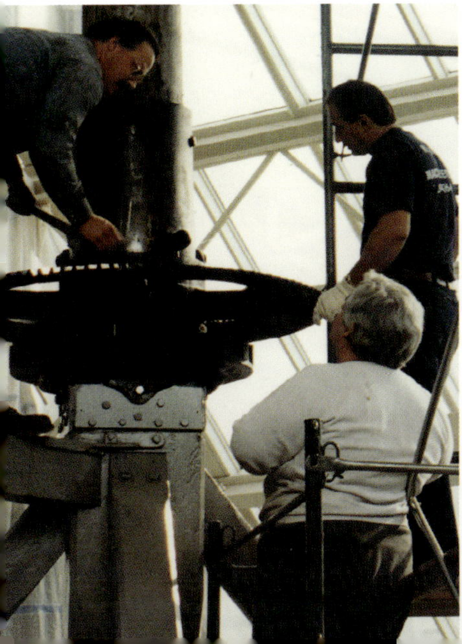

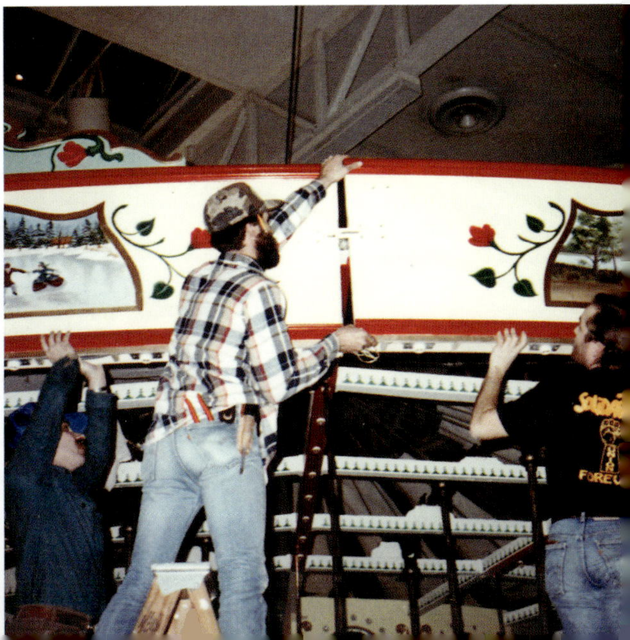

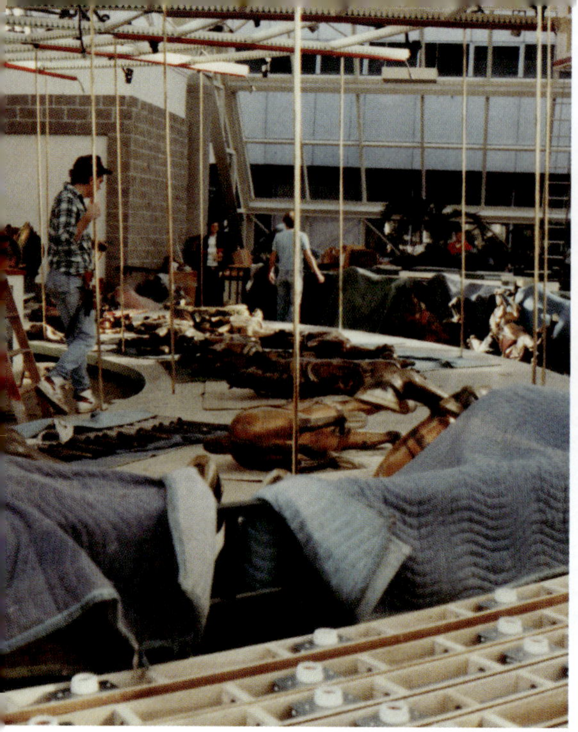

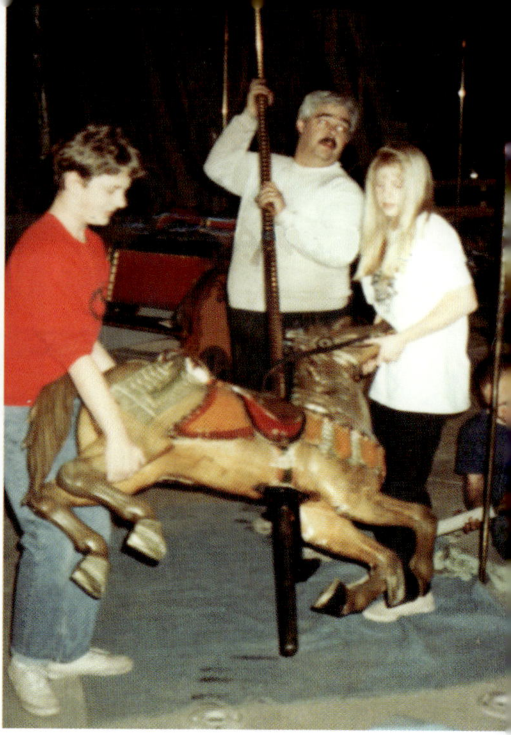

With newly painted and rewired sweeps and spreaders in place, 18 platform sections are suspended from the upper structure while horses and rounding boards await placement. Volunteers Kyle and Chris Killion help Peter Boehm move a horse into position while Art Curtze prepares the telescope which anchors the bottom of the horse. Below, Art Drager works above the sweeps to help hang an outer-row horse.

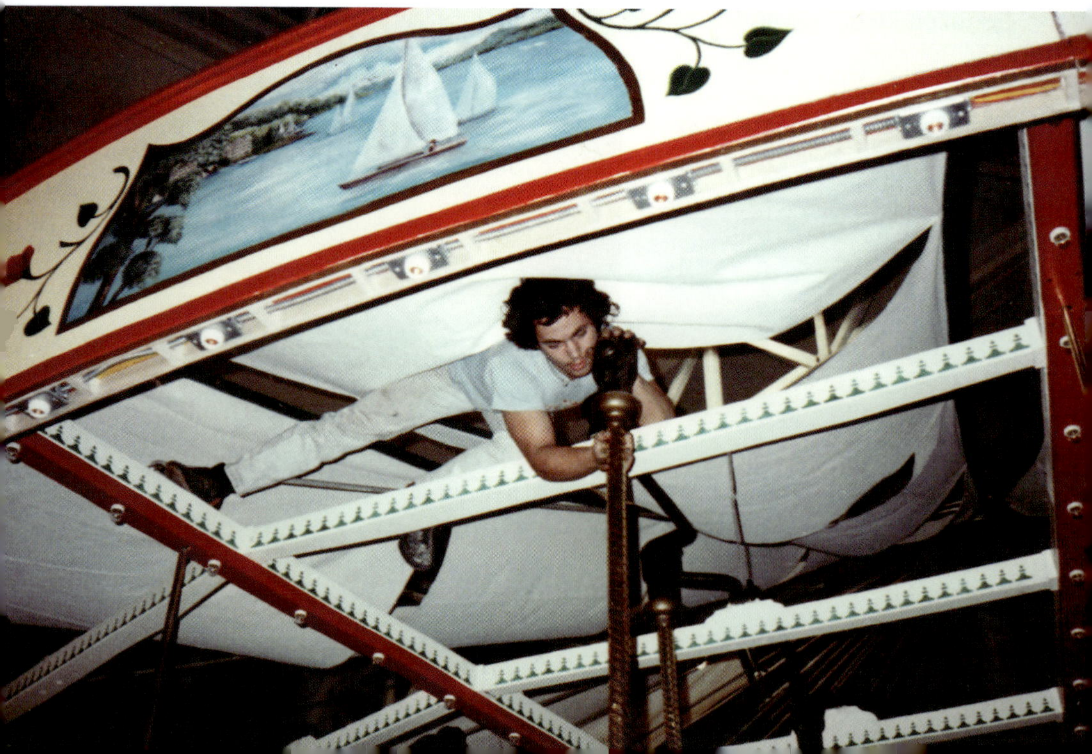

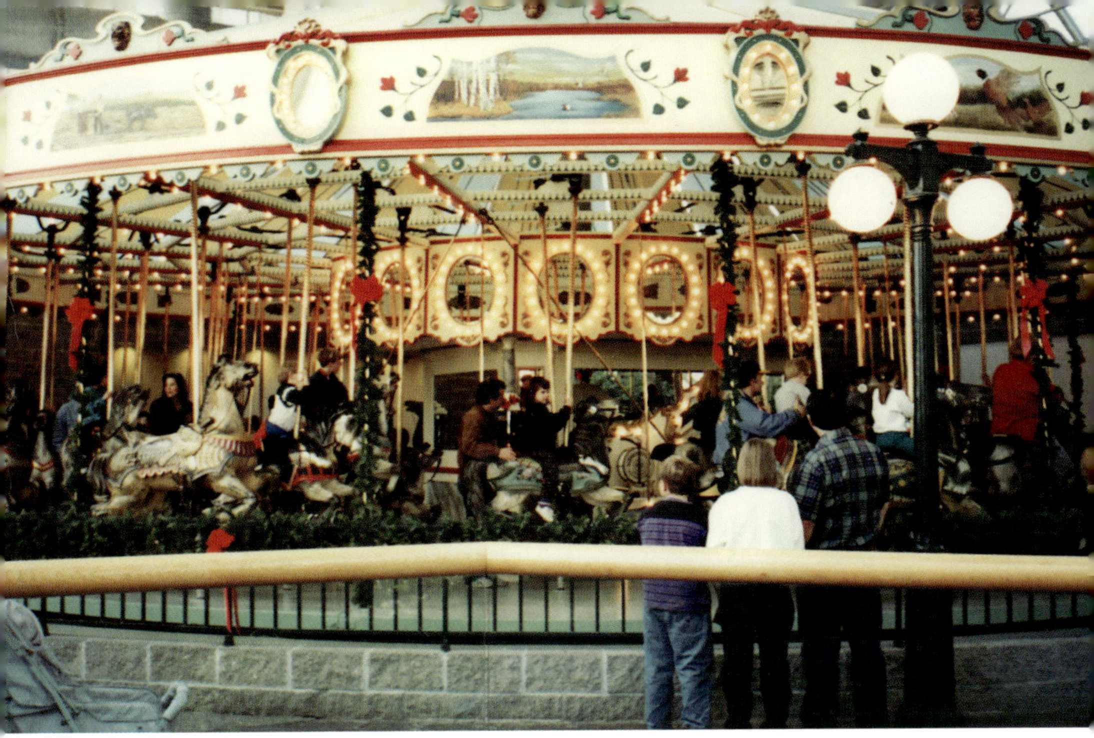

Shown decorated for Christmas, Cafesjian's Carousel drew many riders during its first few years in Town Square Park. The carousel sported a canopy at Town Square, screening riders' overhead view of tall buildings beyond Town Square's glass ceiling. That view, coupled with the carousel's motion, made some riders queasy. People did enjoy the expansive view toward the other side of the park, shown below.

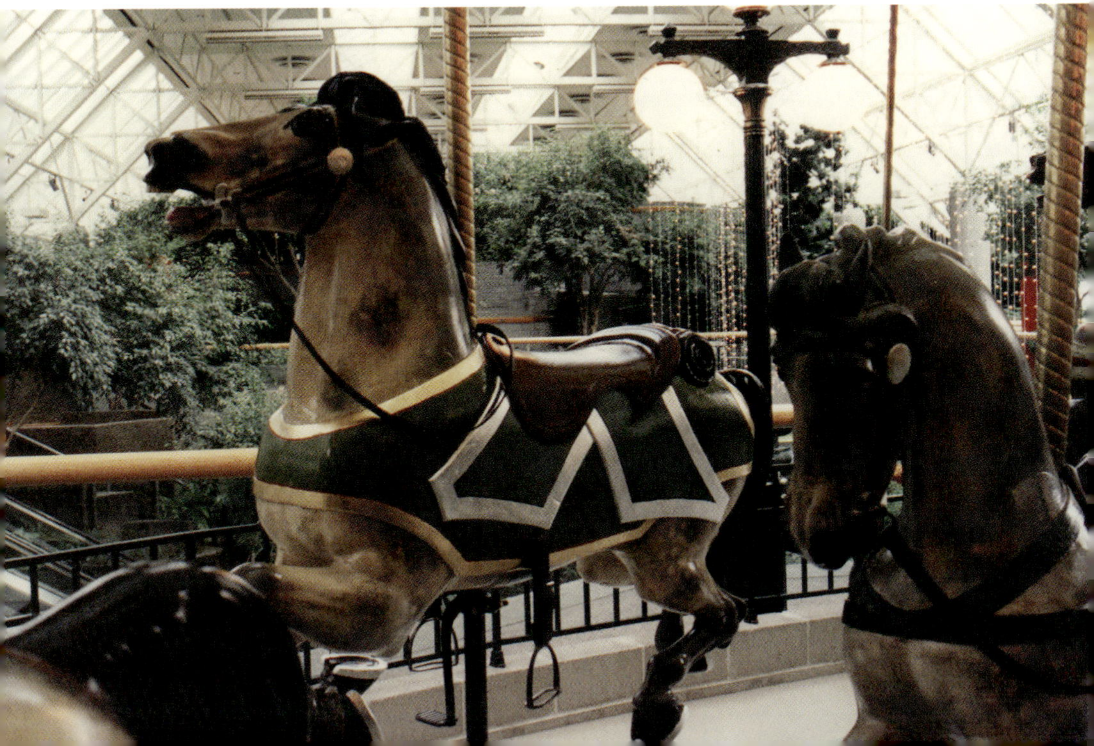

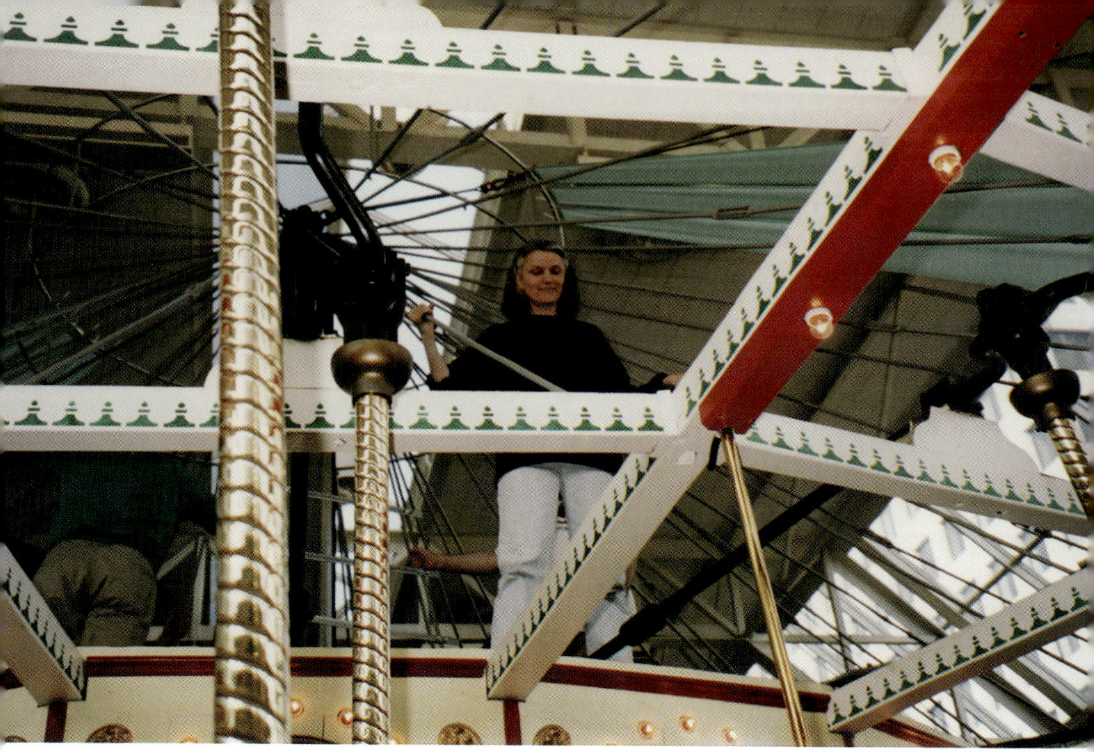

In 1993, Cafesjian's Carousel hosted the National Carousel Association's annual Technical Conference. Rosa Ragan and other attendees enjoyed a rare chance to ride above the sweeps to watch the mechanism work. Below: Cafesjian's Carousel was among the first to modify a chariot to be wheelchair-accessible. Peter Boehm demonstrated how the chariot and portable access ramp work.

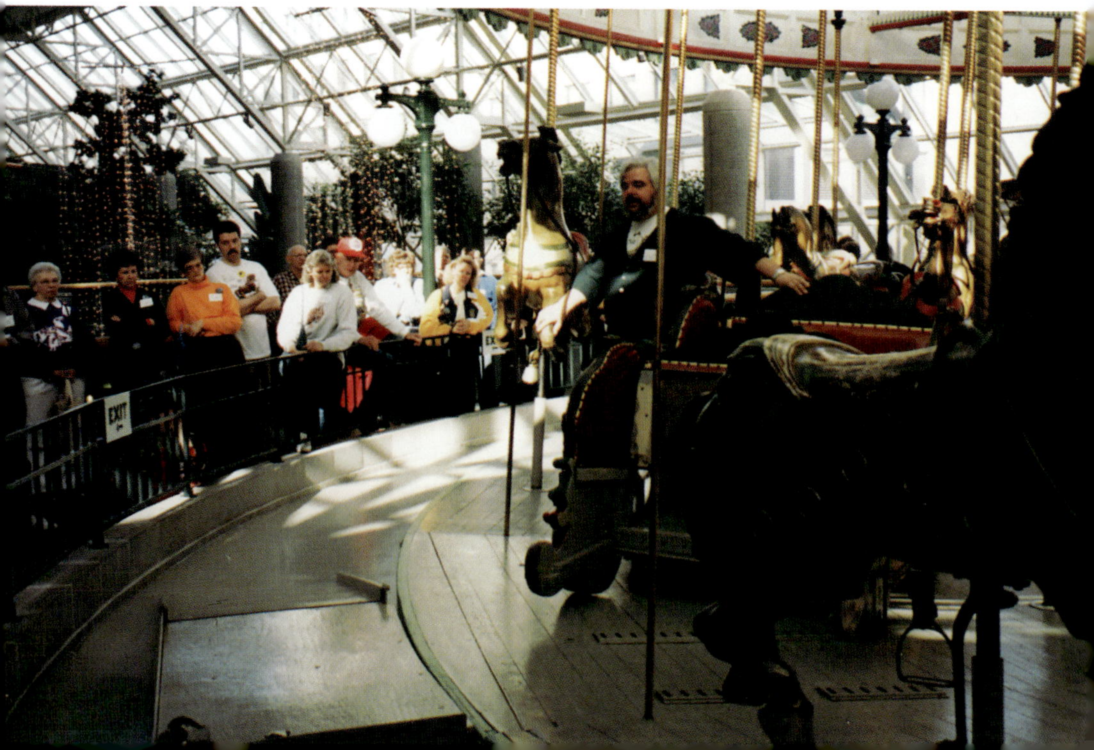

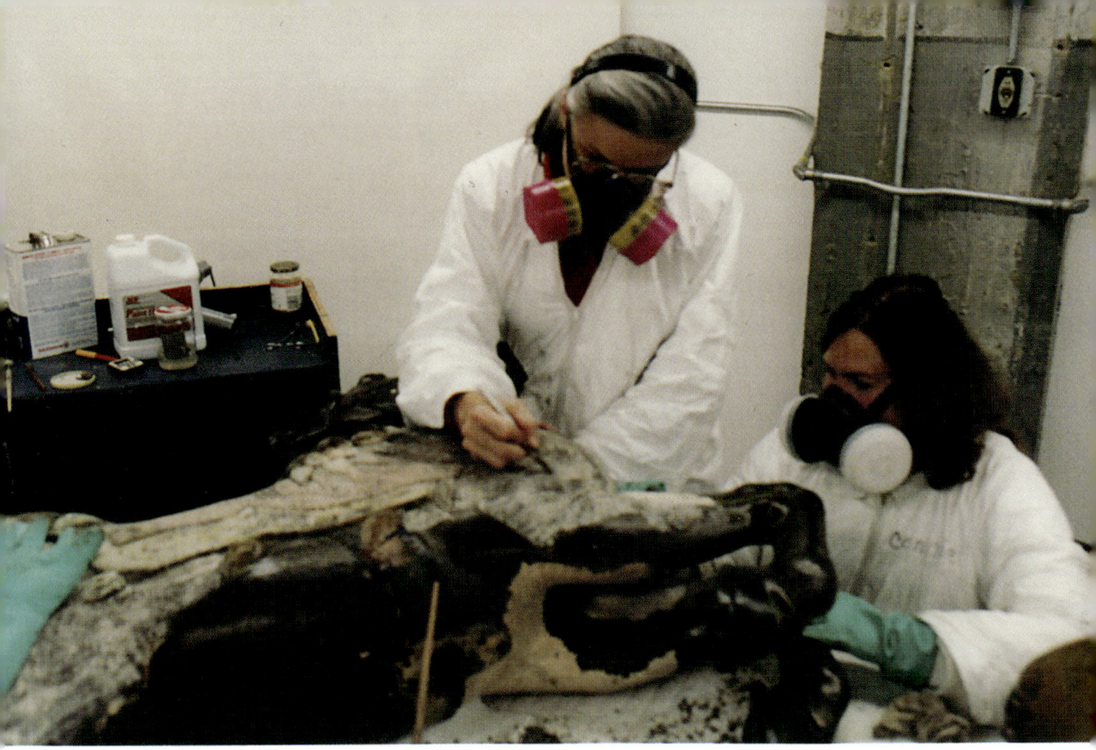

Demonstrating our restoration techniques for the NCA conference are restoration expert Rosa Ragan, left, and Linda McDonald, who took charge of paint restoration after being trained by Ragan. Working in our Lowertown studio, Dick Kenfield, lower left, did much of the wood repair. Audrey Clasemann, right, removes old varnish, leaving only original paint.

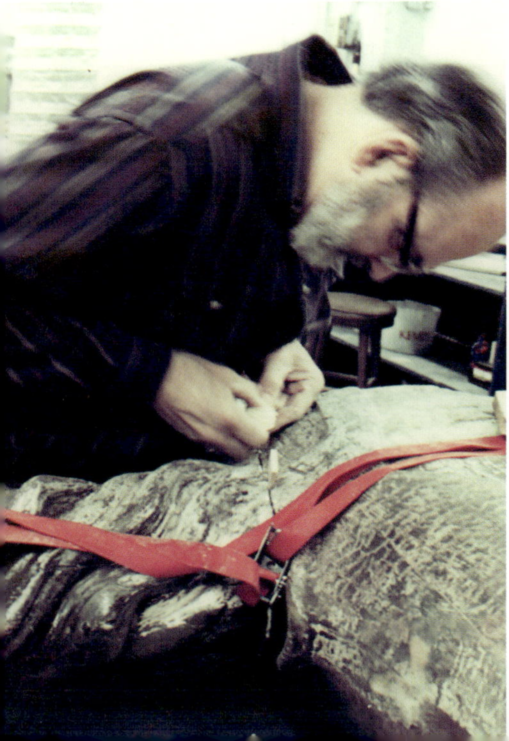

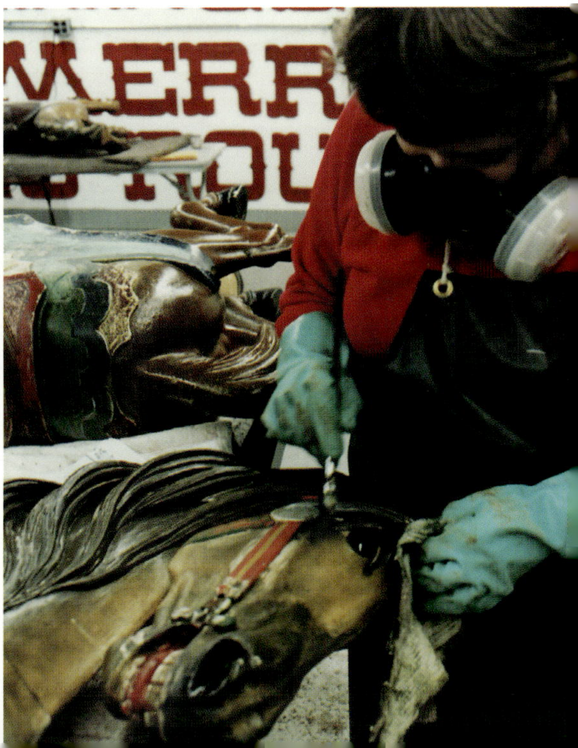

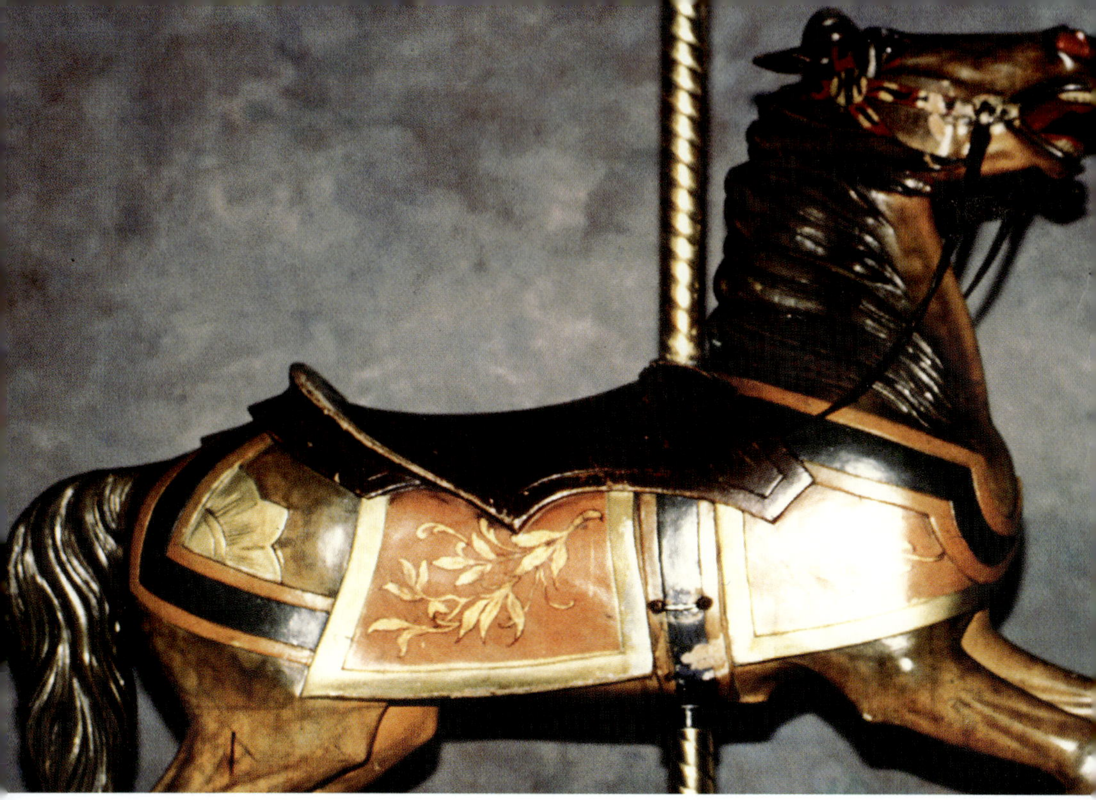

Photographed as they came off the carousel after the 1989 fair, the horses seemed to have brown bodies and dark trappings as shown in the top photo. The lower photo, taken as we began to restore the first horse, shows the contrast between the dark varnish and the underlying colors, such as the dapple gray body, pink saddle blanket, and blue strap. Inset: documentation of each color found. *Photo above by Keith Holland*

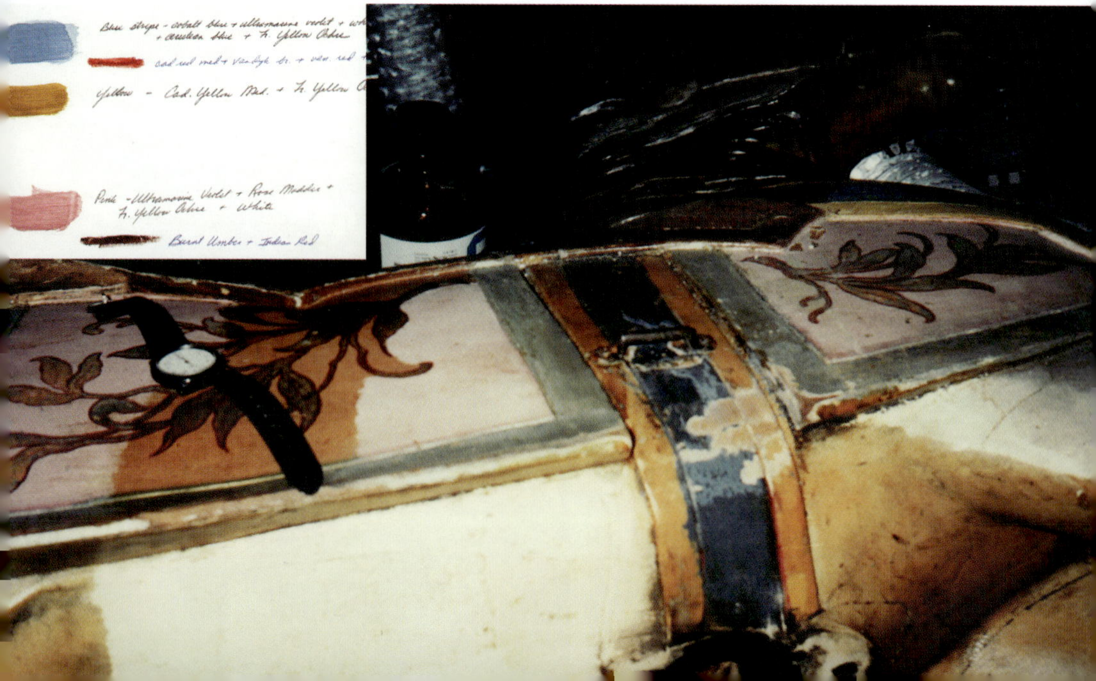

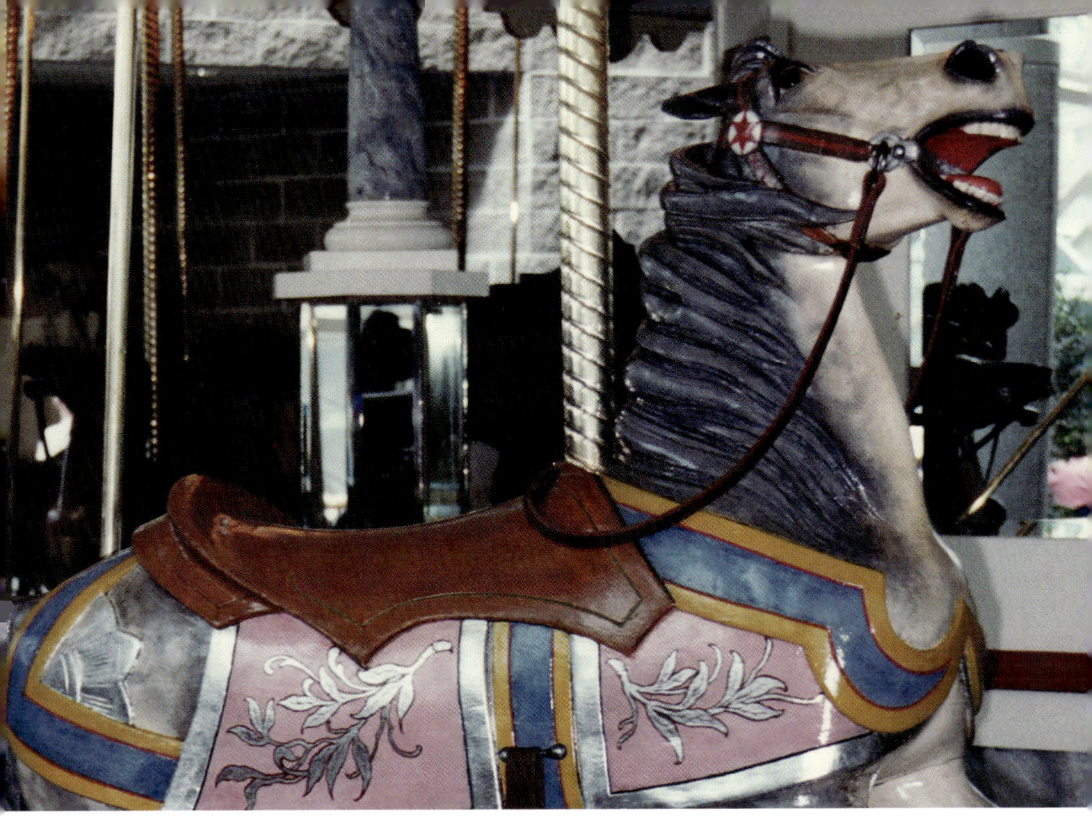

Once the varnish and any non-original paint were removed, each horse got a barrier coat before Linda McDonald inpainted scratched and worn areas. She also applied foil leaf where we found evidence of it. Below, little Katie Garlock waves to media photographers, who came out in force for the unveiling of the first restored horse returned to the carousel.

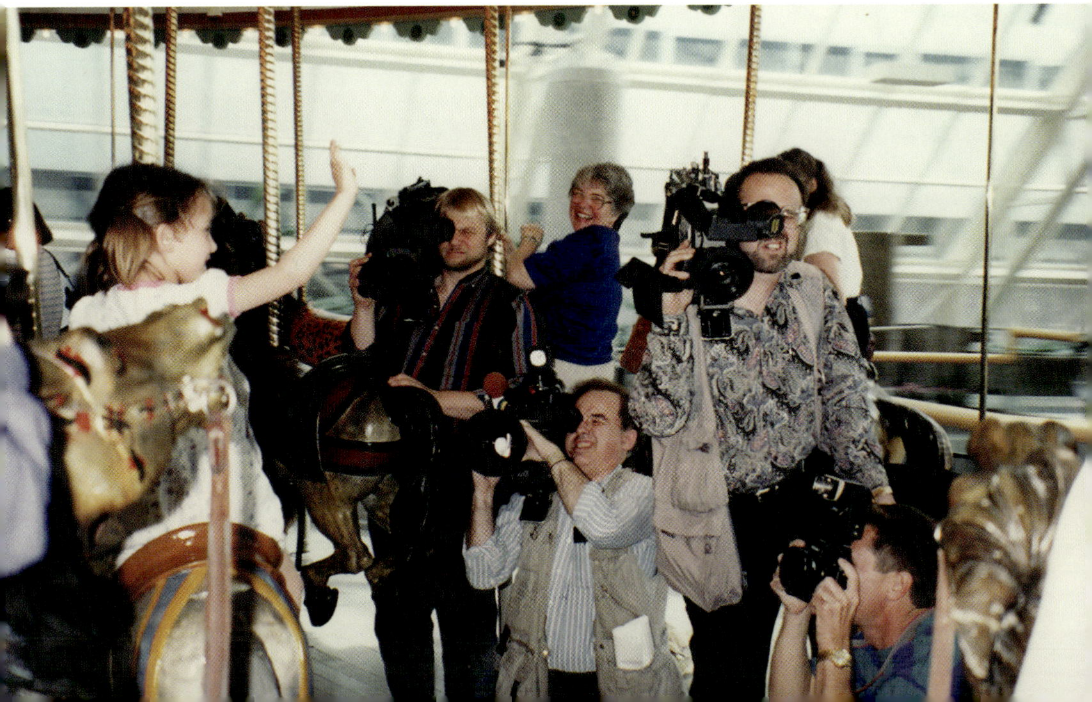

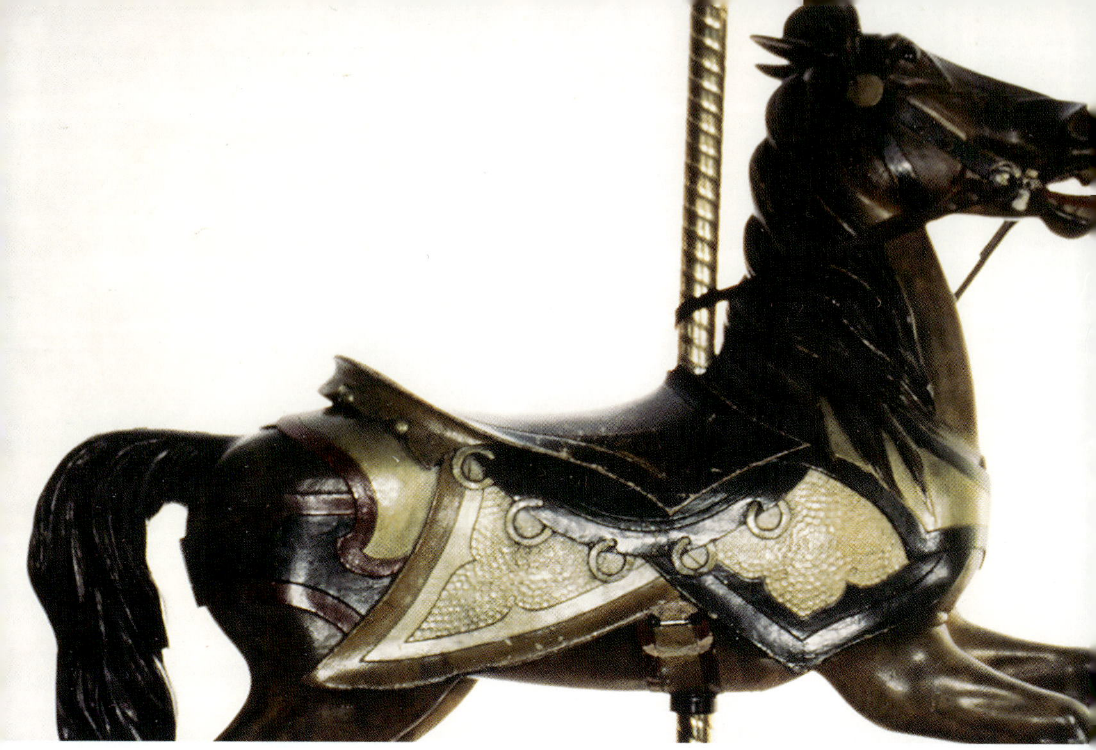

Some of this horse's trappings had been touched up with black paint to cover scratches. The head is curiously long and the eyes too high-set, like those carved at PTC a few years before Cafesjian's Carousel. But the trappings show the carver's attention to detail, with layers of blankets and a sculpted texture to the leafed areas that could be appreciated even under the darkened varnish. *Top photo by Keith Holland; lower by Linda McDonald*

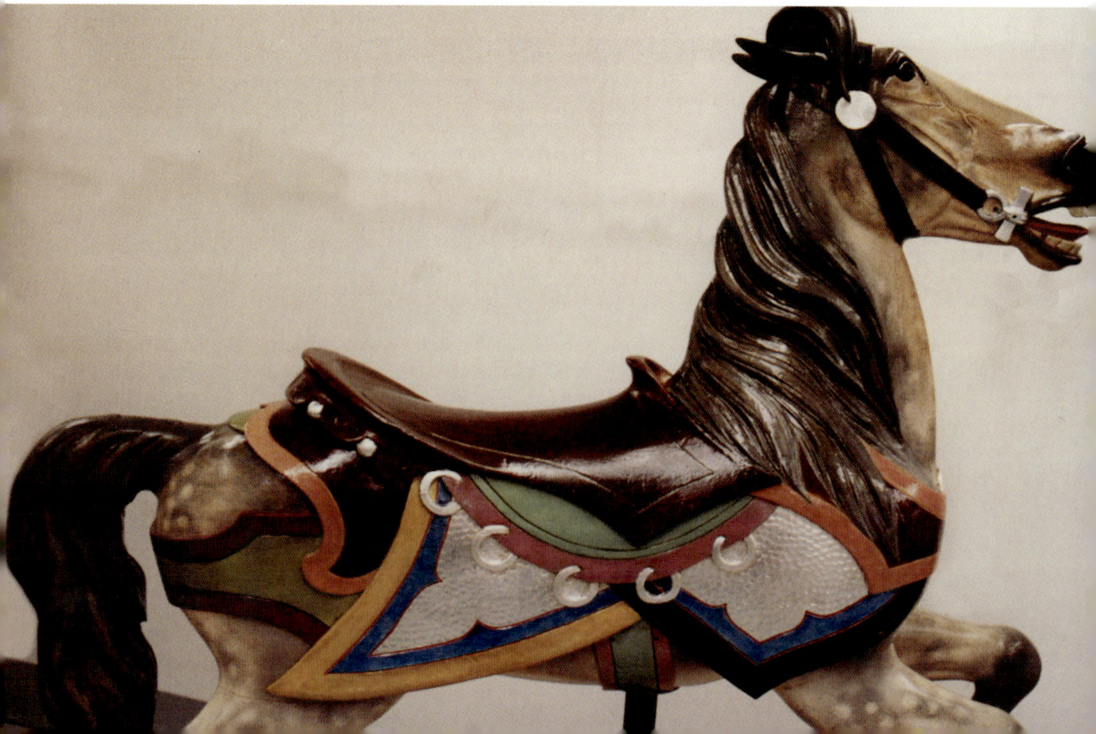

carousel as both art and a community resource. By late November, we had raised $910,000. In addition to Jerry Cafesjian's $600,000 pledge, we had nine others from corporations, foundations, and individuals totaling $110,000. We had nearly $200,000 left from operations at the fair. But with the deadline a month away, we were $390,000 short and that number wasn't moving.

When *Star Tribune* reporter Joe Kimball asked about an extended deadline, Peter said it wouldn't help. People were already aware of the need. We had repeatedly made our case and generated intense local and national media coverage (including ABC World News Tonight, whose reporter Chris Bury had done an extensive story just weeks earlier). "If everybody says no in 1989," Peter asked, "why would they change their minds in 1990?" City council members began looking for a way to pay off the loan without using public funds. But when the loan came due at the end of December there was no plan. It looked very possible that despite 13 months of intense activity, the carousel would be lost.

Just in time, Minnesota Landmarks' David Lanegran stepped forward and offered his organization's help. Minnesota Landmarks had successfully raised millions of dollars from businesses and wealthy families to restore a historic federal courts building and operate it as a cultural center. Lanegran had been very helpful when we began our quest, and he served on our board. He knew Landmarks' credibility and expertise could be helpful. It took an extension to get the deal done, but by the end of February 1990, the city had agreed to make a ten-year, interest-free loan to cover the nearly $400,000 we hadn't been able to raise. We would repay the city out of revenues, and if we had problems Minnesota Landmarks would assist with fund-raising.

There was one more sticking point. Under our original loan agreement, Our Fair Carousel and Saint Paul co-owned the ride. Now, over Peter's objections, the city insisted on being sole owner, though OFC would retain the right to operate, maintain, and restore the carousel. Peter pressed for a provision that nobody thought important, but that would later prove invaluable: if at any time Saint Paul's Town Square Park could no longer accommodate the carousel, the city must provide an appropriate new location within one year. Failing that, full ownership of the carousel would pass to OFC. The agreement was signed March 12, 1990, and as promised, we revealed the identities of our two anonymous donors. At last we could begin preparing the carousel for its new home.

Not many carousels have been disassembled and restored in a way that allowed community members to handle the pieces, give them new life, and put them back into place. In 1990, volunteers did just that, reconditioning the mechanical and structural parts of PTC 33 before moving it downtown. As they cleaned, degreased, stripped, painted, and otherwise transformed hundreds of individual pieces, those volunteers gained a new sense of ownership and pride not only in the pieces they handled but in the carousel as a whole.

For months volunteers gathered every weekend, and some weekdays as well, in a dank Minneapolis warehouse. When this first phase of restoration began in May the floor was still chilly and we sat on packing blankets. As the weather warmed, so did our workspace, and we set up giant fans which mostly circulated hot air and made a deafening roar. Still working through the fall, we were back to warm clothes and hot beverages. What never changed was the smell. A particular pungent odor — a chemical being used somewhere in the building — was our constant companion. We never did figure out what it was.

If you had walked into the warehouse on our first day of work, you would have seen a stack of long metal poles, greasy from 75 years of use, along one wall. In front of them lay old electrical wiring in tangled heaps. Next to that were gears and cranks, the heavy iron parts that make the carousel turn and the horses rise and fall. In another part of the room, rows of wooden beams — "sweeps" and "spreaders" — awaited attention. Largely unnoticed against a back wall were the rounding boards, 18 long strips of sheet metal painted white with red swirls. Commanding attention in the foreground at that moment were 18 large red and white mirror panels and 18 shields painted brown, yellow, and orange.

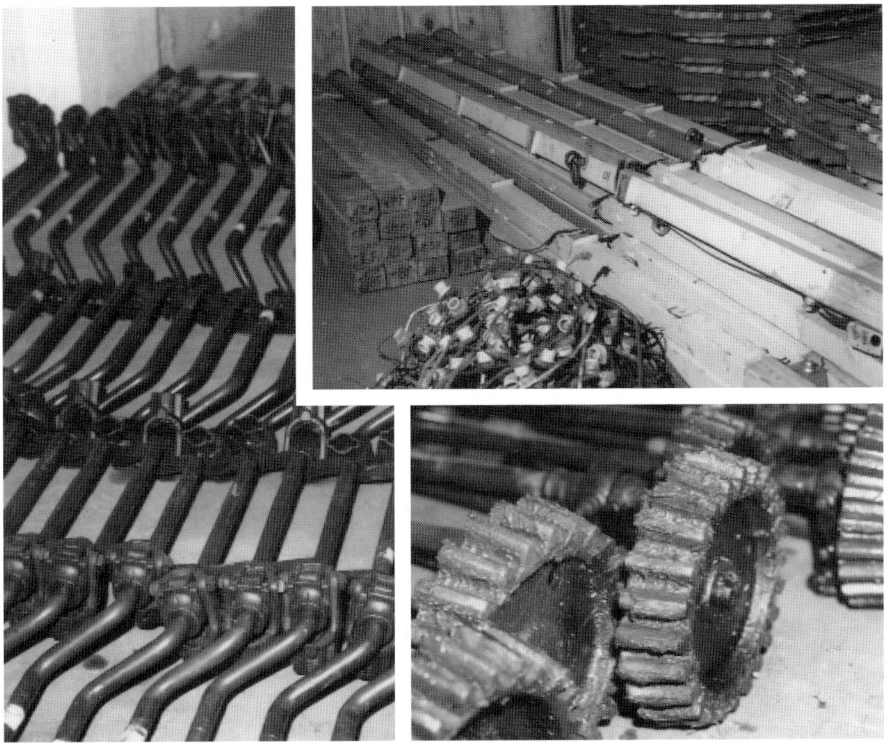

In summer 1990, the working parts of Cafesjian's Carousel were cleaned, repaired, and repainted where appropriate before the move to Town Square.

Peter had organized the parts and the work. The strongest volunteers began to clean the heaviest machine parts while others took apart the decorative shields. Some of these shields were damaged in the 1939 fire, and they had not been repaired. Instead, lights had been removed from all 18 panels, and flat wooden ovals (which reminded us of toilet seats) were nailed in place around each mirror to camouflage holes where the ring of lights had been. We pried off those ovals and cleaned the shields with wire brushes to prepare them for repainting. As we would do with every decorative part, we scraped away patches of paint, down through all the layers, to see what lay beneath. On these shield panels, under the brown, orange, and yellow we found original shades of green and gold. Over the next few weeks, people who could paint with a steady hand would transform the shields to their original appearance.

A similar process applied to dozens of decorative parts, large and small. Large mirror panels needed to have wiring, light sockets, and electrical boxes removed to make way for new ones. A dozen wooden lion's heads, which adorned the crowns over the rounding boards, were readied for repainting. Four more were badly scorched from the 1939 fire and two had been destroyed entirely. We had neither time nor skills to carve new ones, so volunteer Sally Brewer made a rubber mold of the best one and then produced six resin replicas. She made other castings to replace broken decorative scroll pieces and six fire-damaged shields.

Our crew included men and women, boys and girls. They came alone or with friends or as families, especially moms and kids. Everybody there loved the carousel, or came along to indulge someone else who did. For some of the work, we recruited specialists.

When we cleaned grease off the sweeps we found evidence of stenciling that had been painted over. Once we finished cleaning the sweeps and spreaders and painting them their original light yellow, we needed to recreate the stencil pattern. A dozen members of Twin Cities Decorative Artists Guild and Northland Decorative Painters arrived to handle the job. First, stencils were painstakingly cut in a design resembling a row of chess pieces. Day after day each artist laid down a piece of stencil, dipped a brush into a small jar of forest green paint, and "pounced." That is, rather than using a typical brush stroke, they bounced the tip of the paint brush again and again, creating perfect edges and decorating about a mile of beams.

The artists were still pouncing when we made a discovery that expanded their role dramatically. As we looked over some tin panels from the rounding boards, Art Drager, our young mechanic, noticed a spot where some of the red and white paint had flaked away. There appeared to be a figure underneath. Peter scraped away a bit more paint. There was, in fact, a scene under the scroll design. Other panels, too, showed signs of paint under the scrolls.

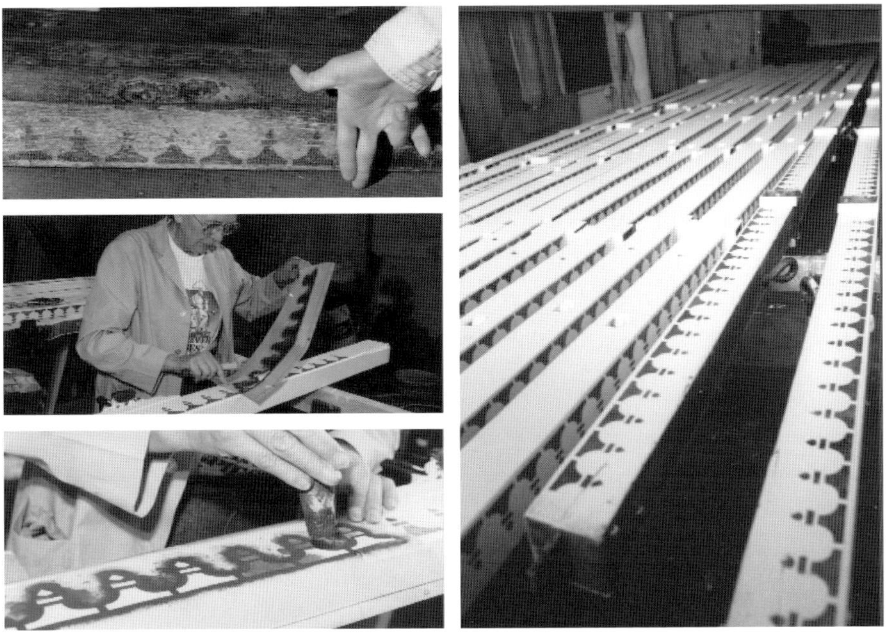

Overhead beams had mostly been repainted, but on one section we found an original forest green stencil pattern (upper left). Artists used a "pouncing" technique to recreate it.

We had been searching for information about the original rounding boards, and this seemed to be a clue. When we finally puzzled out its meaning, the artists would take on a new mission — creating 18 new scenery panels for the rounding boards. Working in the style of PTC's scenery painter, Max Soltmann, they dramatically changed the carousel's appearance. The carousel had been built with simple rounding boards rather than elaborately carved ones, but it had been adorned with beautifully painted scenes. In 1990 these artists brought back that beauty. (We tell the full story of their work in Chapter 7.)

Similarly, members of the electrical industry came together in a big way to update the carousel's lights and wiring. During a media interview on another topic, Peter mentioned that we needed help bringing wiring up to code while preserving the carousel's look. The day the story appeared he got two calls. The engineering firm Gausman & Moore would design the project free of charge. Members of the International Brotherhood of Electrical Workers Local 110 would donate their labor. Through contacts at Saint Paul Technical College, the union also arranged for the necessary metal work, carpentry, and painting to be done by students as part of their learning. The design, which later won an industry award, conceals new wiring within metal boxes that look like part of the carousel's wooden frame. Like the artists, the electricians made something happen that we couldn't have done without them. And like the artists, once the carousel was operating, they brought their families to ride. With pride they would point to the carousel and say, "I worked on that."

We'd hoped to install the carousel in early fall, but Town Square's construction on the space took longer than planned, and the need to create new rounding board paintings complicated our schedule. Setting ourselves a new deadline, we planned a dedication party for the Friday night before Thanksgiving. In retrospect we should have planned the party for well after the carousel was open, to allow for a shakedown period. But we had agreed to the date and the invitations had gone out. The business community, the city, and Jerry Cafesjian all expected the carousel to be operating that night.

We had been reporting to all of them that installation was lagging. Arthur Curtze was in town helping us, and we were both taking time off work. But our volunteers were only available evenings, and many had church and school activities or other obligations. Neither the city nor BCED, the company that managed Town Square, could send anyone to help. A week before the party, we made it official. The carousel would be assembled by the time of the party, but for safety reasons we had to test-run it for a week with volunteers aboard before allowing the public to ride. The foundation under the carousel had been strengthened to support its 30-ton load, but we had to be sure it was handling the vibrations generated when the carousel spun, that the overhead cables were properly rigged, and that all those parts that had just been put back together had a chance to settle in.

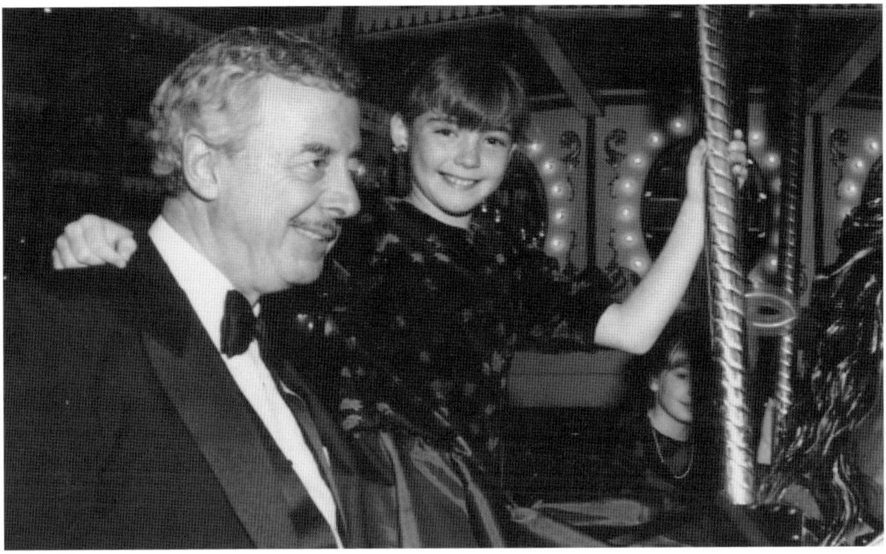

Accompanied by his granddaughter, Carrie Martinson, carousel benefactor Gerard L. "Jerry" Cafesjian unveiled the sign officially naming the carousel for him, and then posed for pictures. *By permission of the Estate of Gerard L. Cafesjian*

Two years earlier our knowledge of carousels came from a single coffee-table book. Now in everything we did we were consulting with wise and experienced experts, researching and using the absolute best practices known to the carousel world. As they would on other occasions, the city and the business community watched their deadlines and grew impatient, and they wondered whether we really knew what we were talking about. Three days before the party Jerry Cafesjian flew in a crew from Carousel Works, a firm in Ohio, to get their opinion of the carousel's readiness. While we continued to place horses on board Wednesday afternoon, two men from Carousel Works inspected the mechanism and said everything looked good. Then they said it needs to run for about a week before you let the public ride.

Thursday evening, the night before the party, the carousel proved the point. With all the pieces together and the horses on board, we gathered a dozen volunteers for a test ride. We had them stand on the platform toward the center of the machine, away from the outer edge. Peter rang the bell and pushed the start button, and in a couple of turns we were up to speed. But before we could celebrate, there was a loud and sudden bang and the tinkle of breaking glass. Peter hit the emergency stop and we all waited nervously for the carousel to come to a stop. One of the one-inch steel cables running from the top of the center pole to a column of the building had come loose, snapping sharply back against the rounding board and breaking some light bulbs just an inch from a mirror. Anyone in the cable's path could have been seriously injured.

The night of the party, the carousel stood still while guests admired its newly painted rounding boards and its lovely surroundings. We hadn't yet begun to restore the horses, but already the carousel looked far more beautiful than it had in its last year at the fair. With his granddaughter Carrie at his side, a tuxedoed Jerry Cafesjian unveiled the bronze plaque that named the carousel and saluted his generosity. We greeted guests and invited them to become volunteers. It was, in fact, a fine party even without carousel rides. The next day we got back to more testing.

The cables had been rigged incorrectly and they all had to be replaced with longer ones. But there was a far more complicated problem, and it stemmed from the center pole that we believe was a last-minute replacement after the original somehow failed during its first day of operation in 1914.

When we disassembled the carousel, we had left the huge center bevel gear, weighing over a thousand pounds, attached to the center pole. Between the gear and the pole were two large iron plates, serving as shims because the inside of the gear was bigger around than the pine pole.

As we reassembled the carousel, we were assisted by millwrights—originally, builders of mills—who specialize in building and adjusting heavy machines. Watching members of Millwright & Machinery Erectors Local 548 at work, we have seen them move the immovable to within the tiniest fraction of an inch. At Town Square, they got the center pole into position, adjusted the bevel gear, and moved on to install the segmented gear, jumping gears,

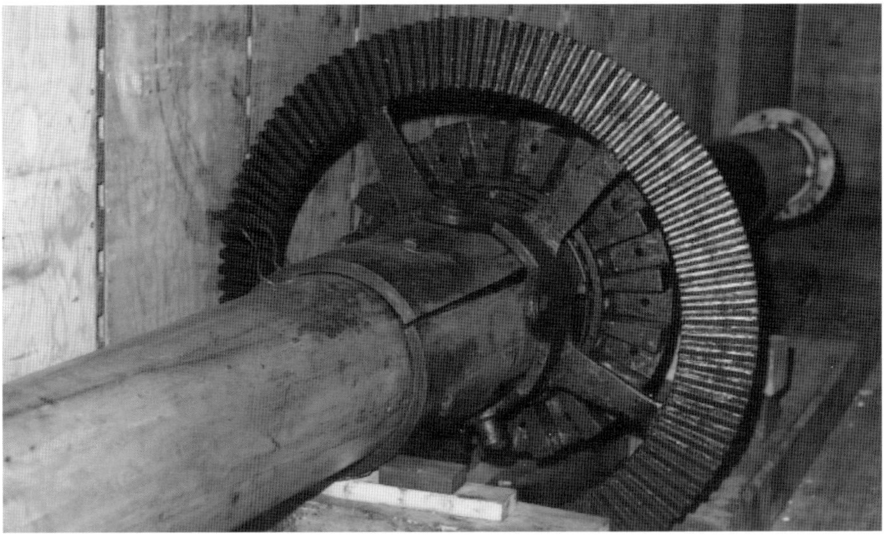

This photo of the center pole shows the attached center bevel gear and the two metal plates between the gear and the pole. The whole assembly was lying in a truck to be moved to Town Square.

and all the other machinery that makes the machine rotate and the horses rise and fall. It was only after our test run that we discovered the bevel gear was not precisely level. Worse, the jumper gears were not moving in a concentric circle with the bevel gear. This is when we realized the center pole was not straight, but banana-shaped, and it was forcing gears to grind together in one part of the carousel's rotation and allowing them to run loose on the opposite side. To prevent catastrophic damage, we needed the millwrights to move the center bevel gear slightly off-center from the pole. The gear, and not the pole, would function as the new center for the spinning carousel.

Had we known this earlier, the millwrights would have had easy access to make the repair. As it was, a three-man crew worked in awkward tight space with all the other machinery in place. They managed to remove each of the iron plates, and using acetylene torches they cut steel shims of slightly varying thickness. Working on the Wednesday afternoon before Thanksgiving, they needed to finish the job before they left so they could be home for Thanksgiving and so we could open to the public Friday morning.

At 2 a.m. Thanksgiving morning, they ran out of acetylene. Two of the men were ready to go home but the third, an imposing guy called "Big Mike" Drimmell, vowed to finish cutting the steel shims "if I have to chew them with my teeth." We waited with the rest of the crew while he made the hour's drive home to pick up a spare tank. The building had gotten cold overnight, and we huddled under packing blankets, which offered little comfort. At 7 a.m., the work was finally finished. The gear was level and the jumper gears were running true. We would return in the evening with a few volunteers to spin the carousel for one final test. Meanwhile everyone went home to get some sleep and eat holiday turkey.

Cafesjian's Carousel opened to the public in Town Square Park on Friday, November 23, 1990, with plenty of media coverage. There was a big crowd that day and again Saturday, and sales were brisk at our small gift kiosk. Set into a carved-out space high in the two-story atrium, the carousel looked right at home.

From the day we first learned about Town Square Park, it had seemed an almost perfect home for the carousel. Town Square didn't have the kind of traffic found at Como Park, but it housed a department store, a handful of small shops, and a food court, and it was a central link in the skyway that connected much of downtown Saint Paul. BCED believed the carousel could be a focal point for activities designed to bring people downtown. They had not only paid to renovate the park, they also made a $50,000 gift to help with our interest payments. We couldn't know that within a few years both downtown Saint Paul and the carousel would be struggling to survive. For the first few years business was good.

As we tailored our operations to the carousel's new home, we had one overriding priority: to strike an appropriate balance between preservation and enjoyment. Everyone had agreed from the beginning that the carousel should be ridden. At the same time, Our Fair Carousel wanted to extend its life for future generations. We often said we hoped it could last another 75 years, if not longer.

Since we would be open year-round, the board decided to conserve the lifespan of the machine by operating just four days a week, Thursdays through Sundays. (We soon learned to expect our best crowds on Saturdays.) We had experienced staff, rehiring Art Drager as our mechanic and hiring Patricia Collis as operations manager. Pat, who volunteered for us at the state fair, had once run a PTC carousel for Royal American Shows on the state fair midway. We began with not nearly enough volunteers but more signed on as we went along. Peter filled in as necessary, and our family worked together almost every Sunday, the three of us taking turns selling tickets, selling gifts, and running the ride.

We developed safety rules to protect against injury to riders and horses alike. To emphasize that this was not just another kiddie ride, we created a pre-ride speech covering the most important rules and touching briefly on the fact that these very old horses are hand-carved and hand-painted. We trained volunteers to anticipate potential trouble: scan the carousel for people who look like they may start wandering on the moving platform, watch people's feet as the carousel slows and try to prevent them from stepping onto a horse's leg. Winters brought a new challenge: snowpants are slippery, and unattended small children wearing them tend to slide. Volunteers learned to spot the ones in trouble and straighten them on their steeds.

The portion of Town Square Park on the other side of the atrium was often rented for weddings and other parties, and we began to rent the carousel in connection with those. This brought in new people, but it taught us that carousels and alcohol don't mix. When people have been drinking, they aren't in a mood to listen to rules, even for their own safety (picture, if you will, six drunken groomsmen deciding to play cowboy). Eventually we decided that if alcohol was to be served, we would rent for only one hour after the bar opened.

A great carousel needs a great band organ. Recorded music can't generate the excitement of a genuine band organ, as was demonstrated during the 1989 state fair when volunteers Mike Merrick and Tracy Tolzmann brought in their Artizan organ for both weekends. The volume made things a little difficult for folks working at the sales tables right next to the Artizan, but everyone in the building marched, or danced, or tapped a foot in time to the lively music.

In 1992, with gifts from Jerry Cafesjian and other carousel board members, we purchased a Wurlitzer 153 band organ built in the 1920s. Board member Mike Merrick found just the right one and spent months meticulously rebuilding it. He undid previous owners' modifications, replaced the original pump with an electric blower, built many parts from scratch, and brought up to code the electrical system for the blower control and lights. The organ could not be restored to original condition; Mike's goal instead was to provide an excellent source of authentic music that would work reliably for this carousel. Band organ experts and carousel volunteers agree that he succeeded.

Mike has made sure we have a varied assortment of music, which comes in the form of paper rolls with holes punched into them. The originals, manufactured long ago, often contain notes that sound jarring because band organs can only play a limited number of notes. The arranger chose a note that was close to the one he wanted, even if it didn't sound quite right. New copies of the old rolls are made using the same techniques and equipment, so the sour notes are perpetuated. But Mike has edited the rolls in our collection, carefully taping over those "off" notes and punching new ones that sound better. It's a laborious way to rearrange music, but it improves the harmony and eliminates those wincing moments sometimes associated with band organ music.

Band organs are loud; they are the perfect instrument to call people to the carousel. The answer to a frequently asked question: No, there is no way to turn down the volume.

When we moved the band organ into Town Square, our volunteers were excited. But by that time the building had already begun a transition from retail to office space, and people working in the travel agency that moved in below us did not enjoy the music. It was a sign of problems that had been building for a while.

The Mall of America had opened in Bloomington in 1992, during our second year of operation at Town Square. As merchants had feared, retail activity downtown began to decline. Within a year, we also noticed this decline at the carousel. Then in 1994, one floor below the carousel, the department store that had been Donaldson's and Carson Pirie Scott closed its doors. Where we once had an enthusiastic line of people ready to ride, we now had an irregular trickle. Months later the Woolworth store in the next block closed and ridership dropped even further. We advertised in *Minnesota Parent* and other outlets, but it made no difference. And when the former department store space was converted to offices, it was clear that retail activity was not coming back.

Now Town Square looked desolate on weekends. Hoping to stir up some activity and make the building a little more welcoming, members of Roseville's Powderpuff Clown Club came to entertain on Sunday afternoons. One beautiful May Sunday was particularly quiet; few people came indoors to ride and by mid-afternoon the place was deserted. The ladies tried to sound optimistic, but Peter told them ridership was so low that we were in danger of not being able to pay our bills. Tears trickled down the face of one of the ladies. "The Day the Clown Cried," as we often call it, was the day we knew the carousel would have to move again.

It was tempting to think more marketing would solve the problem. We met with a marketing specialist who worked with Saint Paul's Parks and Recreation Department. After studying the situation, she made a statement that surprised us: "The carousel is not a destination." It would not, on its own, draw people downtown. That can't be right, we thought. Didn't we have folks who came regularly to ride? Hadn't we based our appeal to the business community on the idea that it *was* a destination? We wrestled with that question until we came to realize that we had brought the carousel downtown to be an *addition* to a healthy mix of attractions, including shopping. Without retail, a family would have to drive downtown, find and pay for parking, and make their way to the upper levels of a semi-dark office building, all for a four-minute carousel experience. It takes more than that to be a destination.

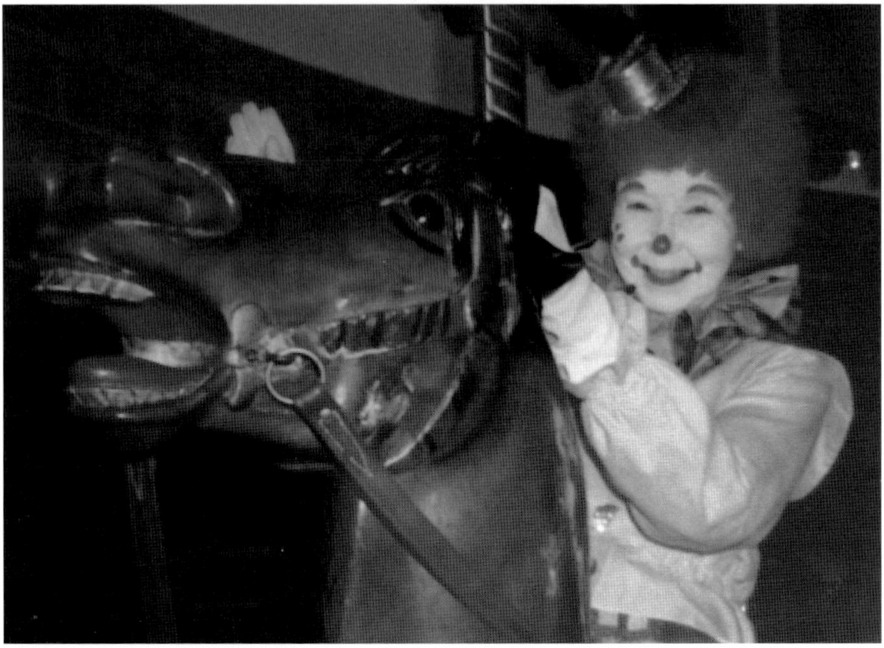

Powderpuff Clown Club members tried to bring Town Square Park to life after retail shops had closed. When the emptiness made even a clown cry, we knew it was time to go.

If it was hard for us to accept that fact, it was virtually impossible to persuade business people and city leaders, including new mayor Norm Coleman. Examining our finances, we told Vic Wittgenstein, our liaison at Parks and Rec, that we were going to have to close soon to avoid going bankrupt. He passed that information up the line. Word came back from the mayor's office: we needed to stay open and do more intensive marketing. We said we couldn't afford that.

We closed in April 1995, but reopened several months later while a consultant hired by the city carried out a marketing plan. The mayor asked Jerry Cafesjian to donate $75,000 to fund the effort, and Jerry gamely agreed. The consultant organized some activities, and for a time there were colorful hoof-prints between the new Children's Museum and the carousel. During this special marketing trial, our ridership dropped even lower than it had been. The city had tried, and we had cooperated, but marketing hadn't helped. So early in 1996 our board again voted to close and to remove the horses for safe-keeping.

The mayor and downtown business interests were not pleased, and they made it personal. There had always been a small group that saw the carousel as a plaything to be exploited. They had never understood how much work and maintenance it takes to keep the machine running and safe, or how much volunteer staffing. They didn't see why we couldn't just give away free rides, or why it was a hardship, as once happened, for a downtown organization to call and demand we open and operate the carousel within the hour because they had promoted a big public event and neglected to tell us. We did. But did you know that someone must climb to the top of the center pole to lubricate the top bearing *every day* before the carousel gives rides? That's one of many reasons a careful operator can't just open the gates and let people in.

The two of us had put ourselves in a difficult position. We both had demanding regular jobs; our schedules were somewhat flexible but our work still had to be done. We hadn't foreseen that running the carousel as volunteers would be like a second full-time job for each of us. The carousel could not afford more staff, and in fact as revenues dropped we had to cut our one full-time staff position to part-time. As committed as we were to the carousel's success, as many hours as we put in every week, it was frustrating to take additional time from our jobs to be summoned downtown for a meeting and pay for our own parking, only to be told we weren't working hard enough.

When Peter spoke up to explain the limits on the carousel and its volunteers, word went out that he was difficult to get along with. He was willing to live with that — he was passionate about the carousel, he spoke his mind bluntly, and he seldom worried whether people liked him. Even Nancy was sometimes shocked by his audacity, but we both knew a timid approach would not save the carousel. Still, when the same group decided to blame Peter for the carousel's lack of traffic, it made no sense. Stores were closing because people weren't coming downtown. Nobody attacked the head of Carson Pirie Scott when they turned out the lights.

The head of the Building Owners and Managers Association wrote an opinion piece for the *Pioneer Press* saying the carousel shouldn't be allowed to leave; we hadn't done enough marketing and should have been open more days each week. Nancy wrote an opinion piece in response saying, in part, that all our marketing efforts cost more than they generated, and that when you are losing money every day, being open more days doesn't help. The group had helped BCED fund the renovation of Town Square Park, so they felt we owed them something. But we were a nonprofit organization with no reserves, verging on bankruptcy. We weren't about to let the organization go under.

Even before we closed, we began urging the city to let us move the carousel to Como Park. If the carousel wasn't a destination, then it needed to be part of something bigger. The 1914 carousel would nicely complement the 1915 conservatory, and it would provide another family-friendly activity. But Mayor Coleman was focused on revitalizing downtown and determined to keep the carousel there. Twice we were called to meetings at which he proposed new downtown sites. A building housing an old theater on Seventh Place was being considered for multipurpose renovation. When that fell through, there was a plan to house the carousel in a Children's Museum annex, in an alley where riders would be surrounded by the backs of tall buildings. Our board said no, thank you. We had worked too hard to accept a bad location.

At one point the mayor and his chief of staff seemed to believe that Peter was advocating for Como Park in defiance of the rest of the board. They began calling board members, sounding them out. One Saturday morning, the mayor called Lorraine Kenfield at home. She told him she thought Como Park was the right location. He said he was "99.9 percent sure" that wasn't going to happen. "Oh good," Lorraine said sweetly. "Then there's still a chance."

Twelve months after we closed the final time at Town Square, no viable location had surfaced, and the city had no new proposals. The 1990 agreement between OFC and the city said if this happened OFC was entitled to become the carousel's sole owner, so in 1997 we began the process of asserting ownership. After several

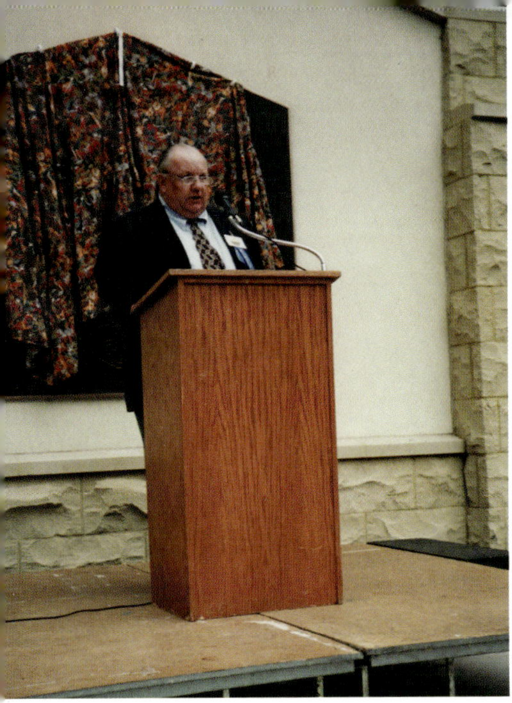

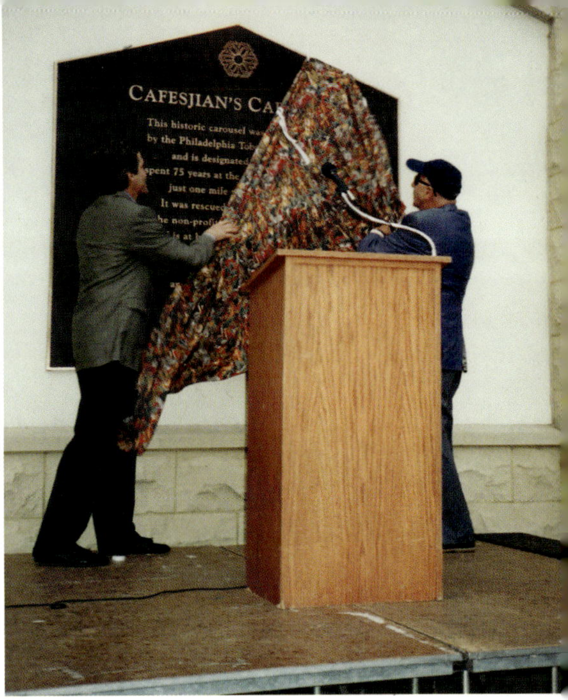

A grand opening in June 2000 celebrated Cafesjian's Carousel's new home in Como Park. Praising the teamwork that brought the carousel to Como Park is Vic Wittgenstein of Saint Paul's Parks and Recreation Department. Wittgenstein forged a new partnership between OFC and the city, paving the way for a new carousel pavilion in Saint Paul's most popular park. At right, Mayor Norm Coleman and Jerry Cafesjian unveil the sign that tells the carousel's story. *Photos above by Barbara Deneen*

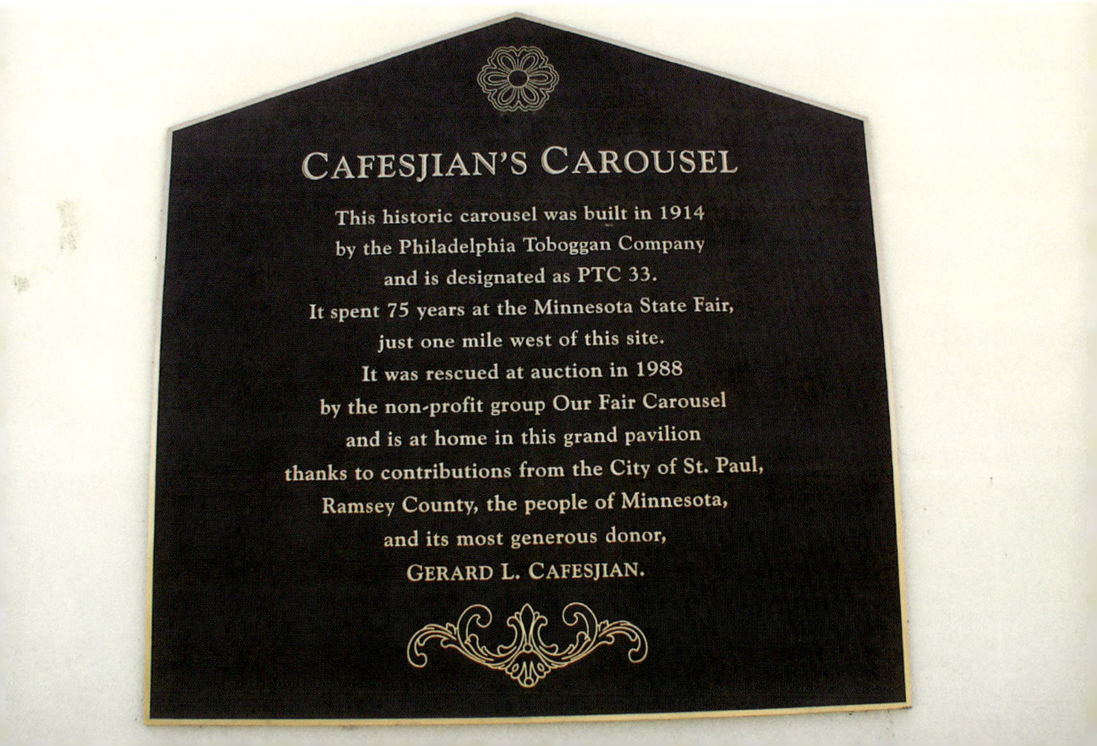

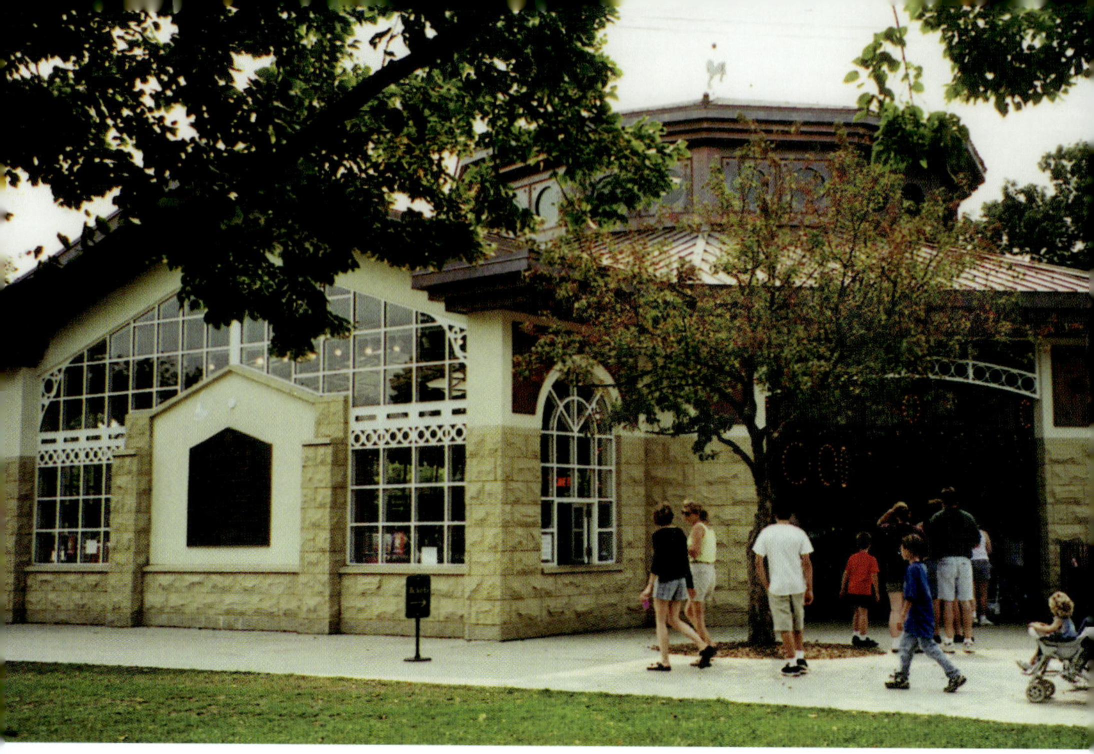

The Cafesjian's Carousel pavilion, built for $1.1 million, features a copper roof, simulated stone siding, a clerestory that admits light from above, and eight garage doors fitted floor-to-ceiling with windows that provide a view of the carousel even when it is not operating. For the grand opening first ride, Cleo Cafesjian rode the alligator horse, her favorite, and Jerry rode next to her. *Photo below by Barbara Deneen*

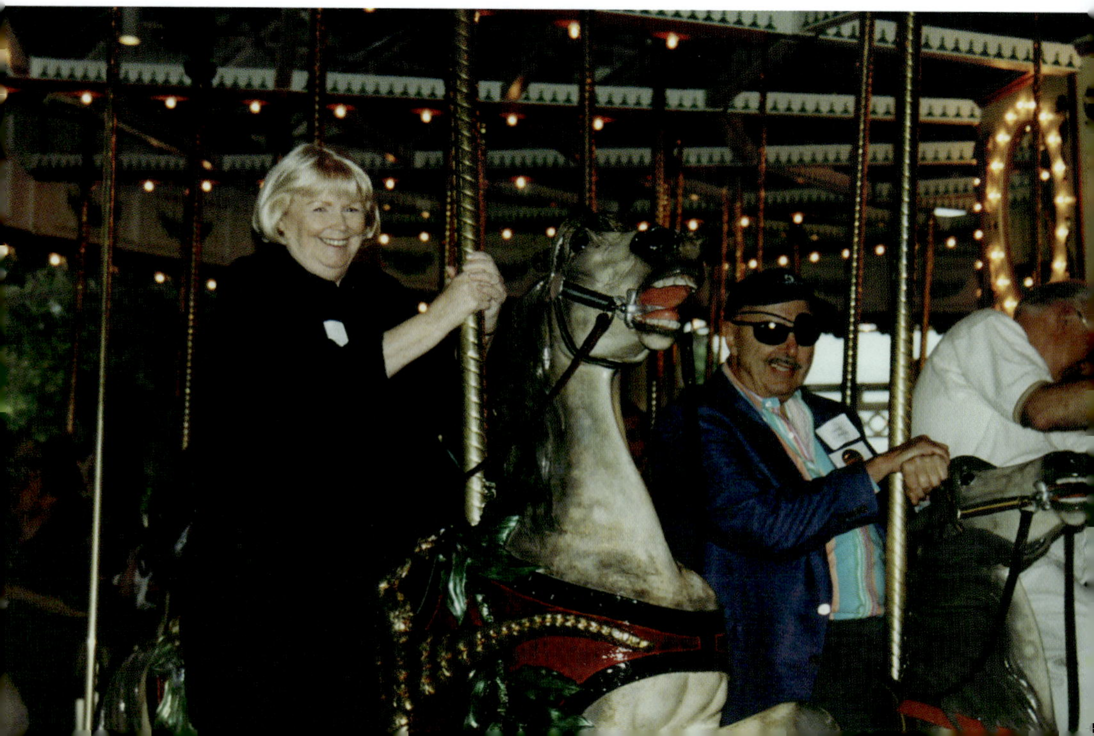

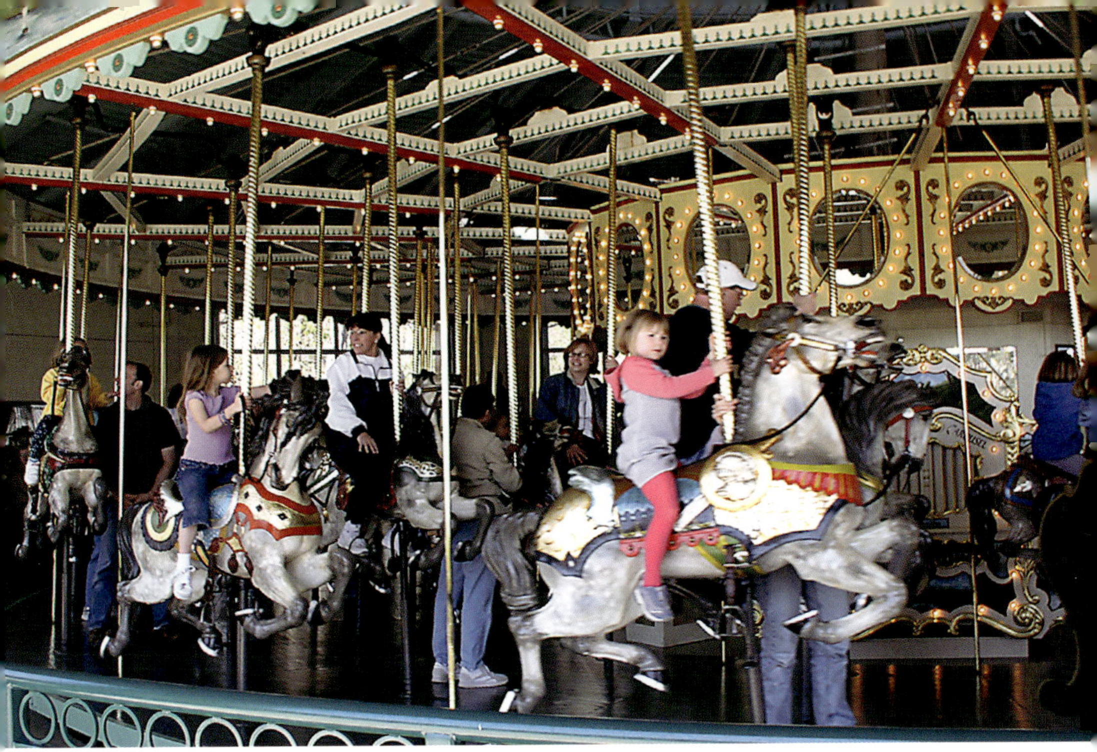

The Cafesjian's Carousel Wurlitzer 153 band organ was extensively rebuilt and restored by Mike Merrick, who continues to maintain it (inset). The façade was painted by Linda McDonald. The organ uses dual-roll frames; one roll continues to play while the other rewinds. The Wurlitzer replaces the carousel's original band organ, which was destroyed by fire in 1939. *Organ photo by Mike Merrick*

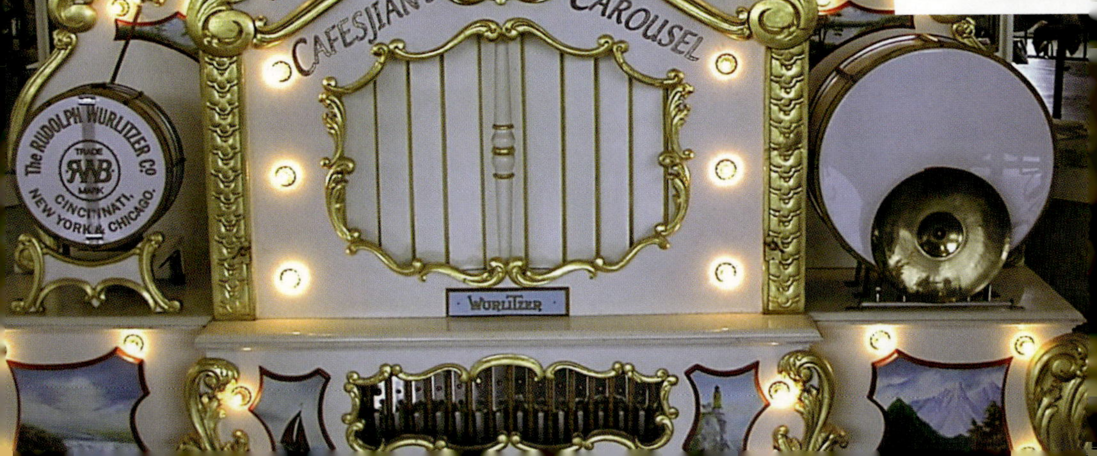

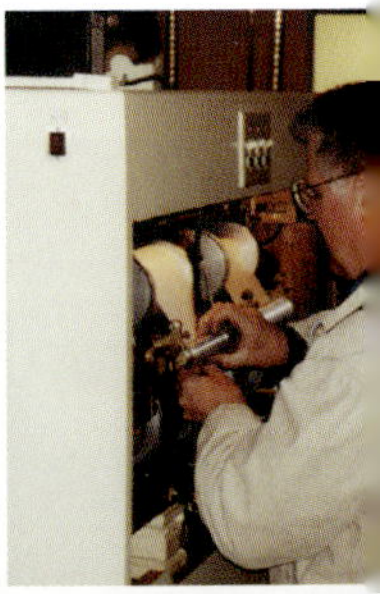

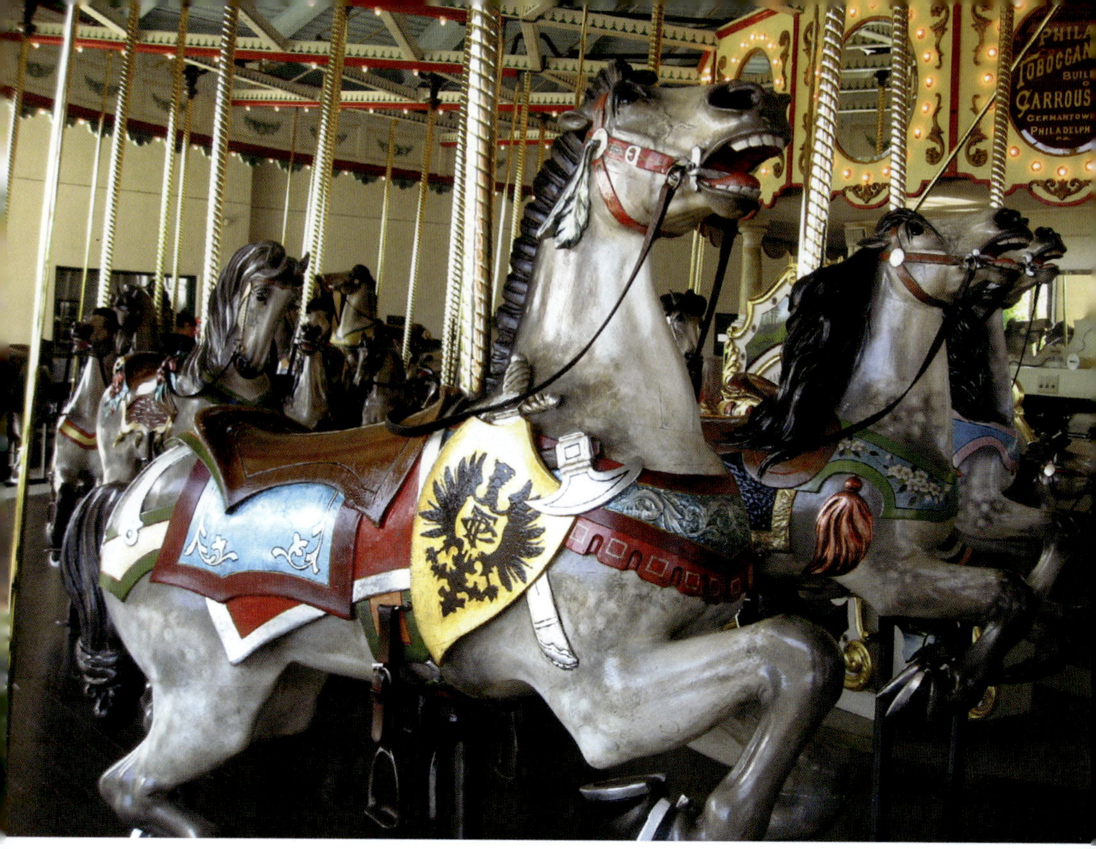

In keeping with tradition, the lead horse carries a shield bearing the logo of Philadelphia Toboggan Company. Linda McDonald, who restored all 68 horses, each year carefully touches up scrapes and scratches, leaving the original paint protected by a clear barrier coat.

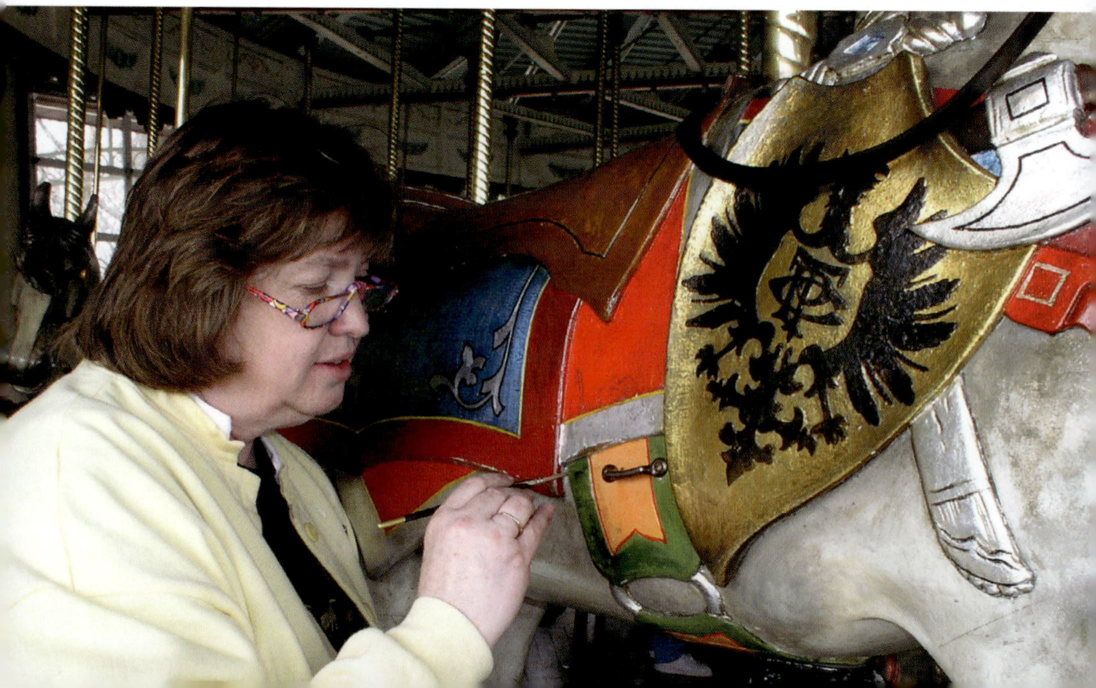

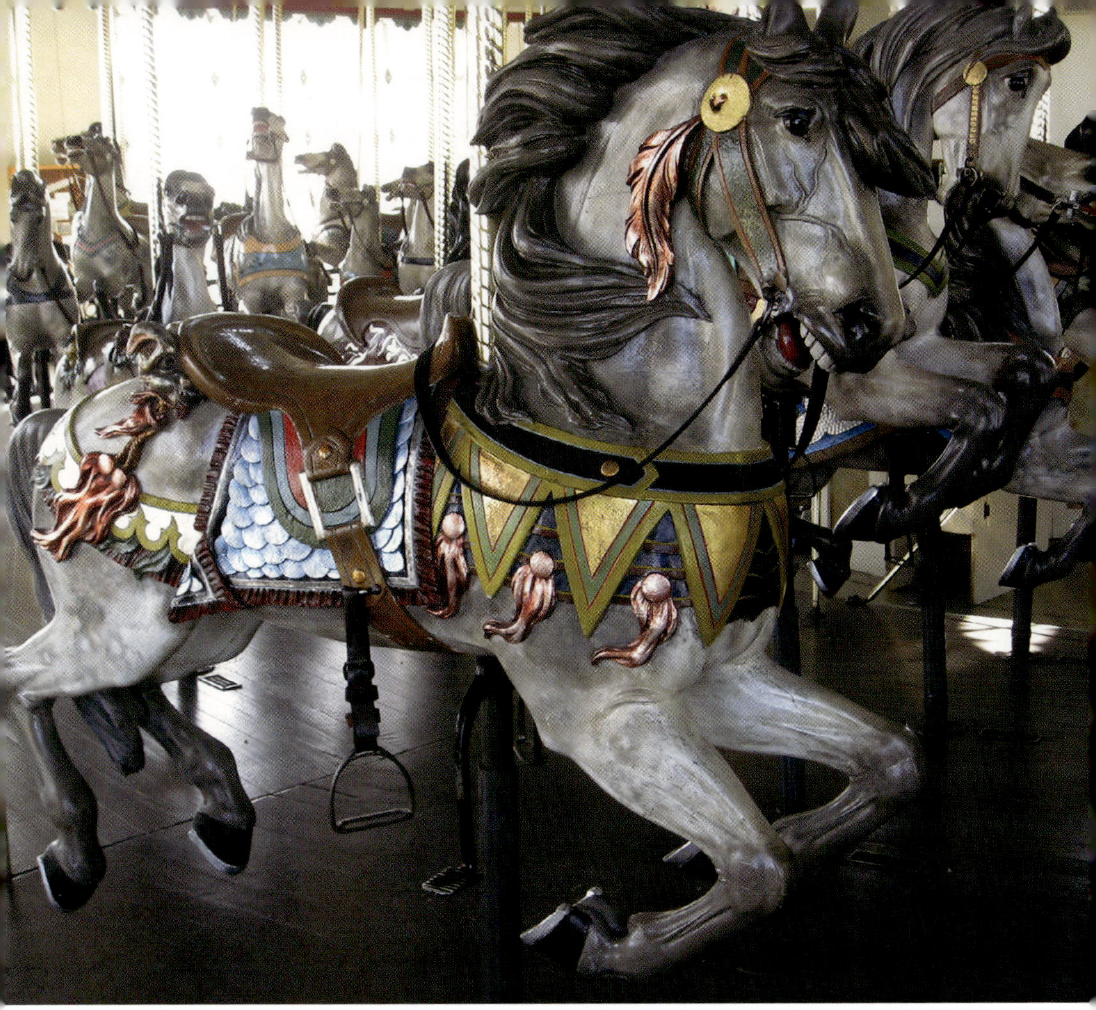

Three horses carved by the famed Charles Carmel are aboard Cafesjian's Carousel. They illustrate classic Carmel features including animated expressions, windswept manes, armored chest straps, slender bodies, and prominent fetlocks. PTC purchased these in 1913 after Carmel suffered financial losses.

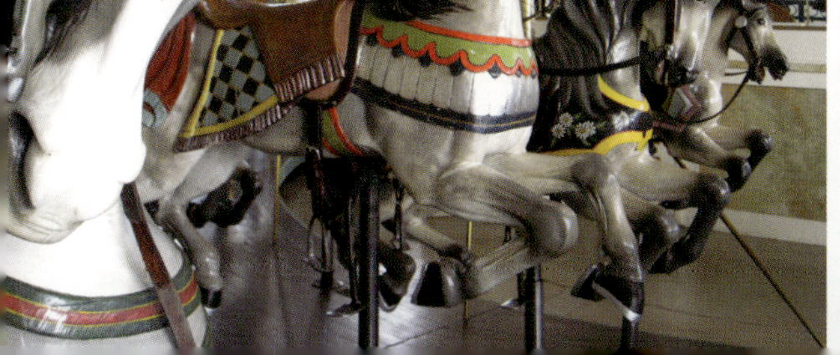

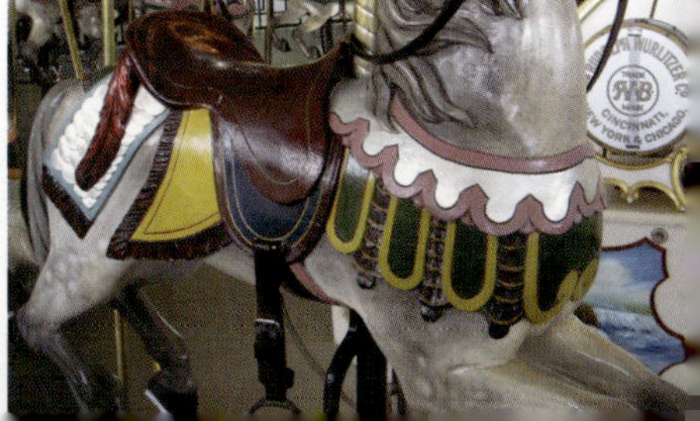

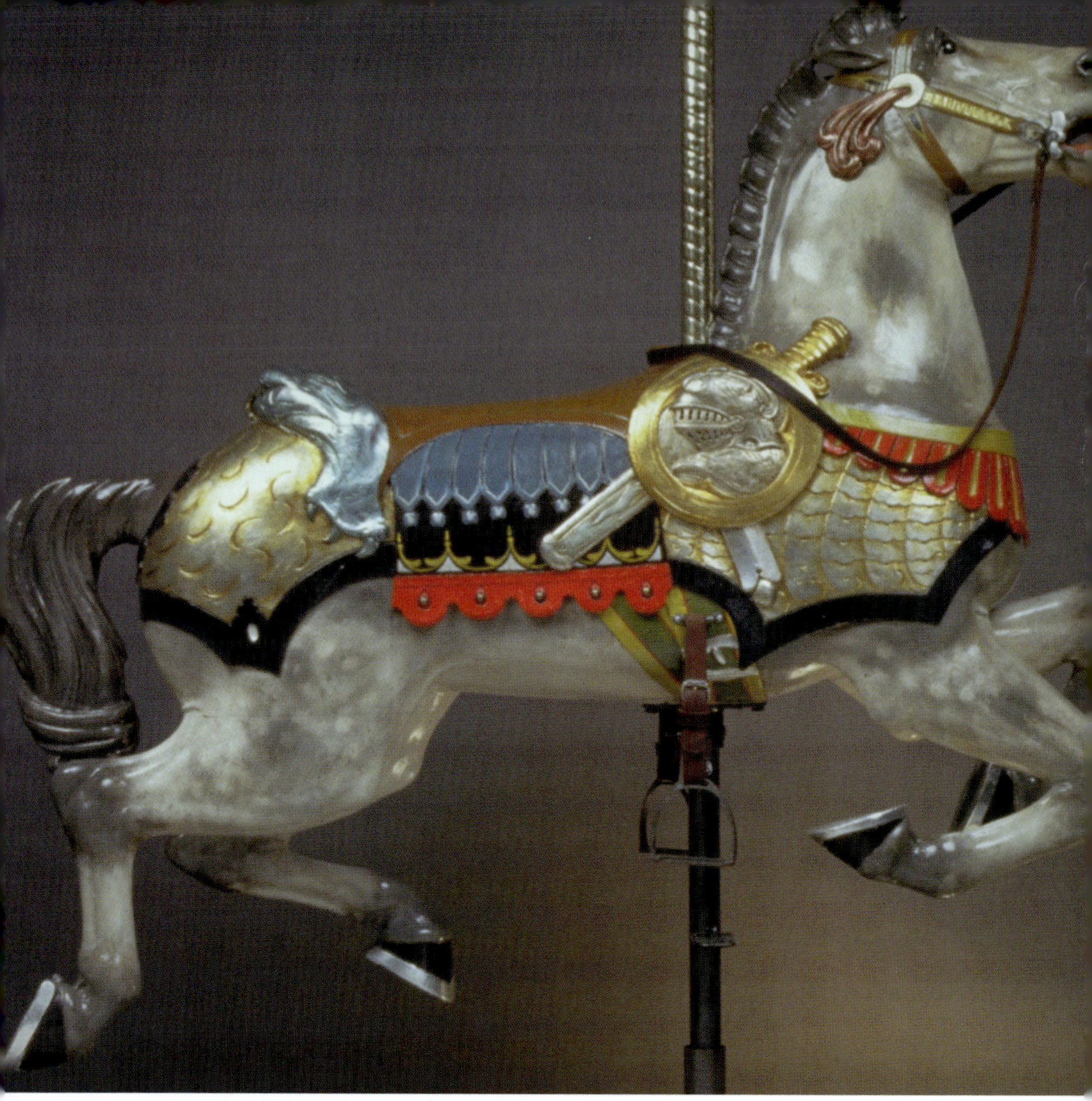

Like the lead horse, this knight's horse has a roached mane and armor. Riding opposite one another on the carousel, each leads a rank of seven outer-row horses followed by a chariot. Lower left, heads were "brightened up" with red and black paint by earlier owners. *Upper photo by Jerry Mathiason; lower photos by Linda McDonald*

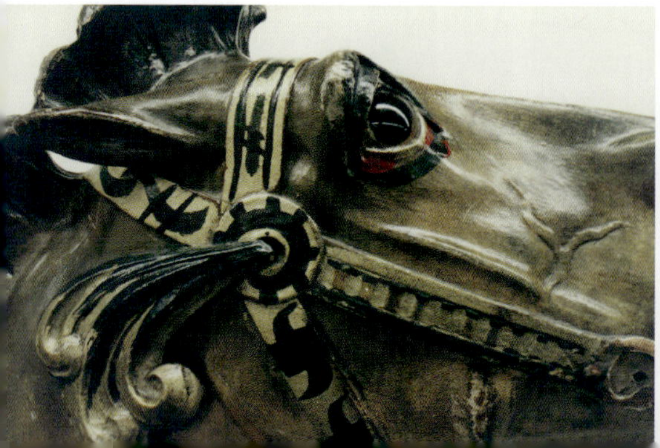

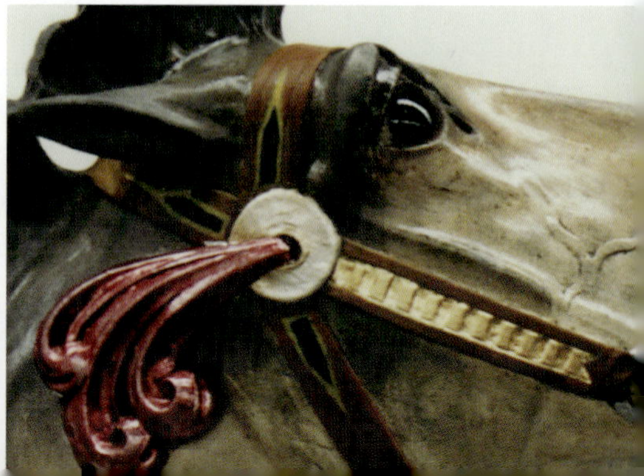

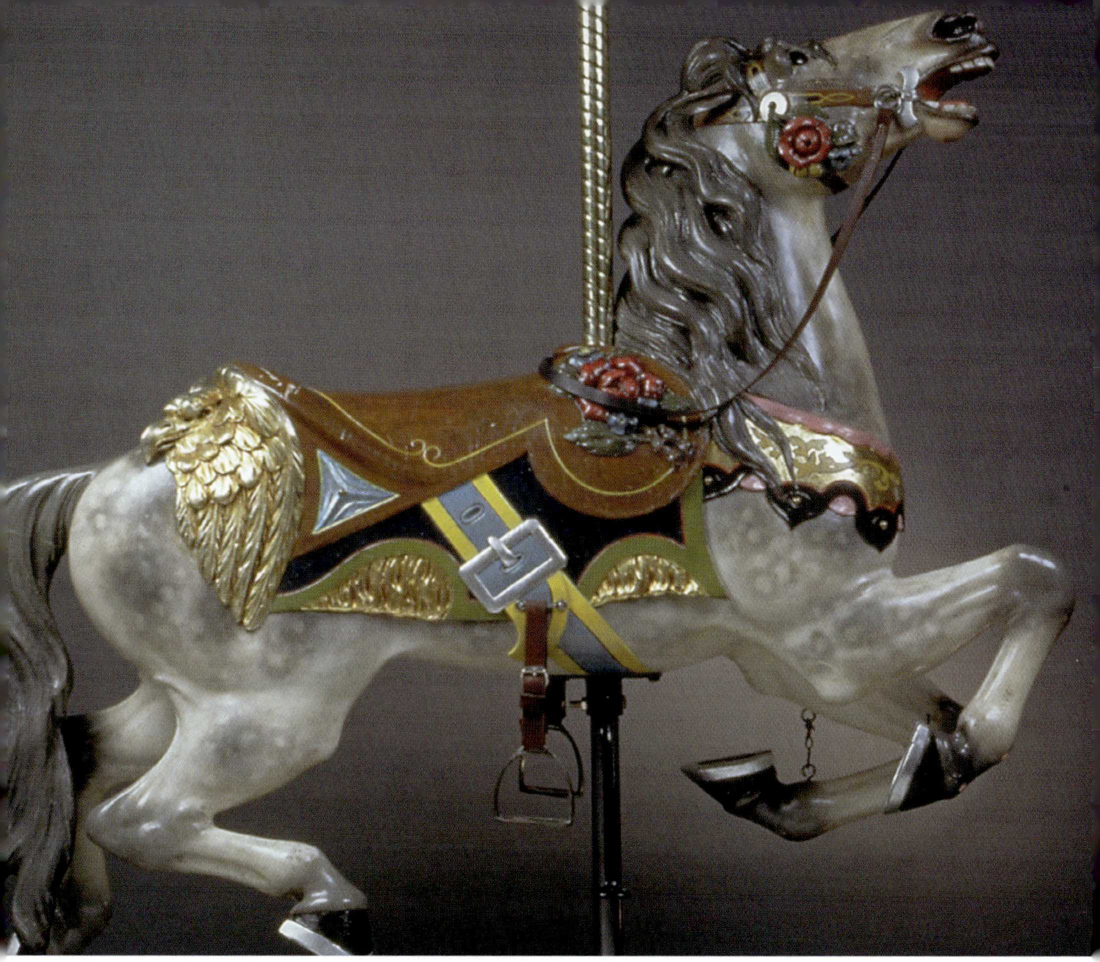

This golden eagle is a beautiful example of how PTC carver David Lightfoot adorned the cantle, especially on outer-row horses. Note attention to anatomical details. During restoration, Dick Kenfield repaired the left front leg and put back the makeshift chain first used by a long-ago restorer. *Upper photo by Jerry Mathiason; lower photo by Linda McDonald*

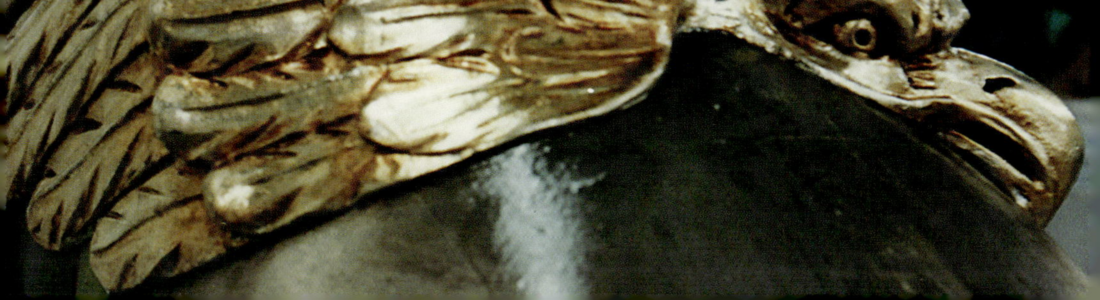

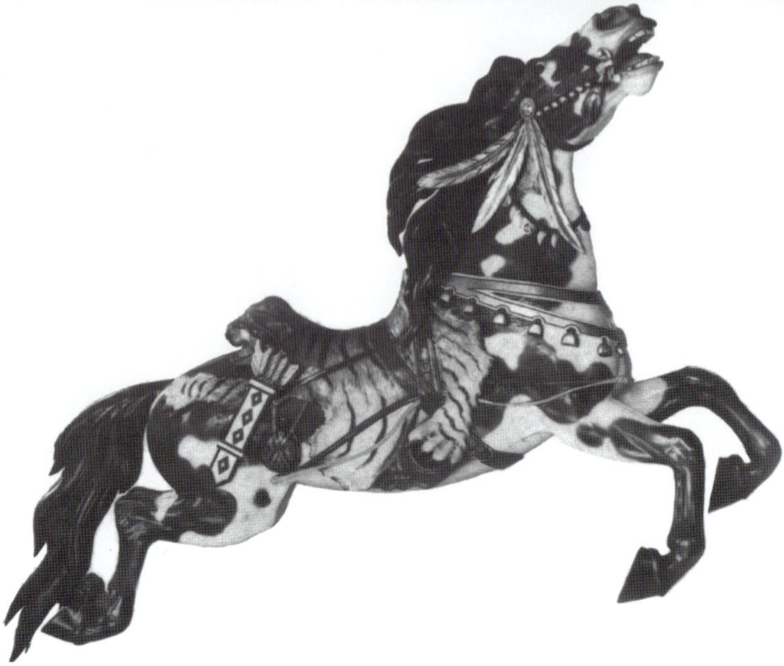

A leaping PTC pony, circa 1908, was among the few photos collected by carver David Lightfoot. In 1914 he replicated its trappings on a horse for PTC33 and had painter Gustav Weiss make it the one pinto in a dapple-gray herd. *Upper photo from the collection of Marjorie Maben-Briel*

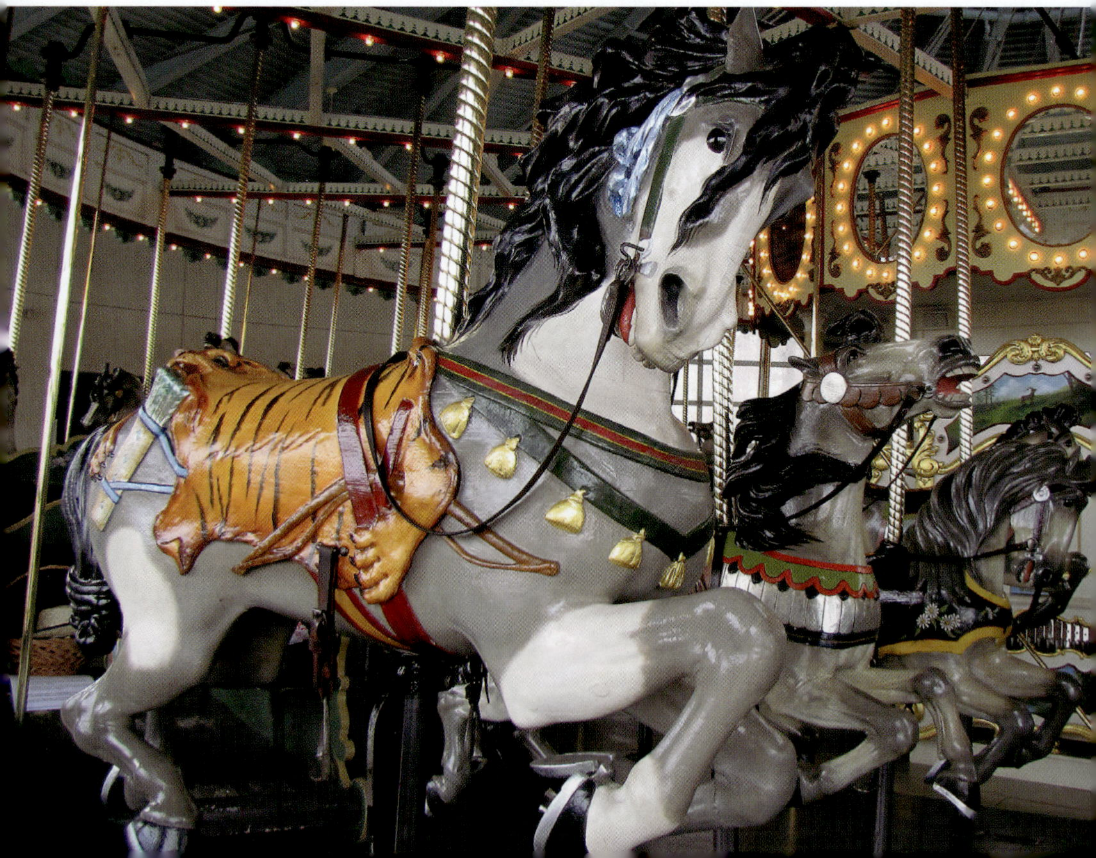

delays, the city accepted that the conditions of the agreement had been met, and paperwork was quietly signed making Cafesjian's Carousel the property of Our Fair Carousel, Inc.

We had been restoring the horses, and they were looking beautiful. Now we just needed a place where they could be ridden. With board member Keith McCormick chairing the selection committee and Peter keeping a low profile, Our Fair Carousel solicited proposals for a new location. We received three, from the Minnesota Zoo, the Minnesota State Fair, and the City of Saint Paul. City officials had realized that if they wanted the carousel to remain in Saint Paul, they needed to make their strongest proposal. At long last, they invited us to put it in Como Park.

The OFC board evaluated all three proposals carefully. The zoo was attractive because it drew the most visitors over the course of a year, but we would need to cover the cost of a building. In addition the zoo was relatively distant from the carousel's original site and a long trek for our volunteers. The state fair had been the carousel's long-time home, but there, too, we would have to pay for a building and we could only operate 12 days a year. At Como Park we would be just down the street from the carousel's original location, and while a new building was necessary, the city and county would contribute toward its cost. Jerry Cafesjian, too, favored Como Park and was willing to contribute toward a pavilion there. The committee recommended Como, and the board agreed.

We had dismantled "the old state fair carousel" and moved it from the fairgrounds in October 1989. Exactly ten years later, in October 1999, we finished installing Cafesjian's Carousel in Como Park and testing it with volunteers aboard. When the weather turned sunny and warm, we started up the band organ, opened the doors, and tried out our new building for a few days. Then we closed up for winter, confident that the carousel was beginning a new decade — and a new millennium — in the right location.

7

Tin Panels and Painted Ponies

The 68 horses on Cafesjian's Carousel are clearly the stars of the show. People who fell in love with them at the Minnesota State Fair could see their beauty, even through park paint and discolored varnish. But what a pleasant surprise to discover that these brown horses were really dapple gray (and one pinto), with elegantly painted trappings and a considerable amount of foil leaf! How nice to see their broken parts carefully repaired, and above their heads, the unexpected surprise of 18 scenery paintings. Our Fair Carousel began the restoration process in 1990 with the frame and mechanism, and then we spent most of the decade restoring the horses. Our goal was to make the carousel look as much as possible like it did in 1914, but with signs of wear appropriate to its age.

The rounding boards presented a mystery. We knew that rounding boards on Philadelphia Toboggan Company carousels all had delicate scenic paintings by the same man, Max Soltmann. We had no photographic evidence that such paintings ever adorned PTC33, but we had a single anecdotal clue. While we were setting up the carousel at the fair in 1989, an older man came to speak with Peter. He said he'd worked on the carousel after the 1939 fire, and he remembered paintings of scenery on the rounding boards. He knew that some were destroyed, but he'd seen other, less-damaged ones taken off and stashed in a basement of one of the big fair buildings. He couldn't remember which one. Peter spent days rummaging in dusty corners under buildings like the coliseum and hippodrome, only to learn later that during the 1940s those basements were cleared out and used to store war supplies.

By the time Our Fair Carousel acquired the machine, the rounding boards had been painted with a red-and-white scroll design. In summer 1990 as we began to restore the frame, we discovered pictures under the scrolls. When Peter saw that there were paintings on these panels, a part of him hoped these were, in fact, originals. We began to scrape away at the top layers to expose what lay beneath.

The images we began to uncover were crudely drawn, cartoonish. Soon we could see that they were not Max Soltmann's work. But could PTC have paid someone else for them? Checking the company ledger, we found our answer. Max Soltmann was paid for scenery paintings for PTC33; these images were not original. The ledger also told us that Soltmann's paintings were on pressed-wood-fiber panels, something like Masonite. They would have been damaged not only by the fire but by the water used to put it out.

Even knowing that these tin panels were not original to the carousel, we needed to see them. We began a tedious process of removing the red and white paint from all 18 panels. It clung stubbornly to the paint beneath, and neither chemicals nor hair dryers softened it much. Meanwhile, the paint underneath was soft, so when we scraped at the top layer we often went right through to the metal surface. Wearing face masks to protect against lead, we and our volunteers scraped away for weeks. This was not going to be easy.

The pictures that emerged, painted on tin, were pastoral scenes: a family farm, a north woods setting, children on a swing. Subjects like these typically appeared in Soltmann's carousel paintings. We concluded that when many of the original pressed-wood panels were heavily damaged by fire and water in 1939, manager Lew Hoffman replaced them all with tin. He needed to get the carousel patched up and operating quickly, and he wouldn't have brought in fine artists. Instead, we believe, he hired sign painters and told them to do their best to represent the *subjects* of the original paintings. Fifty-one years later, we also had a tight deadline and small budget, but we were committed to restore the carousel to its 1914 appearance. What to do?

The answer was right in front of us. A group of artists, members of the Twin Cities Decorative Artists Guild and the Northland Decorative Painters, were creating seemingly endless stenciled patterns on the sweeps and spreaders. We asked them: would they create 18 new scenery paintings in the style of Max Soltmann? They would. First, using the themes we had uncovered, watercolor painter Carol Hegerman developed full-size sketches in Max Soltmann's style. To supplement her sketches, she brought in armloads of art books marked to show examples appropriate to each scene — how the sky should look, how people dressed, how horses were depicted. Guided by these materials, the artists painted directly on the tin panels, which we had sealed and primed. We asked Linda McDonald, a member of the group, to do some finishing touches to ensure that the panels would all look like the work of a single person. Working together and generously leaving their work unsigned, the artists transformed the rounding boards from a 1950s carnival ride to a work of art, our best effort to recreate the carousel's original look.

On the other hand, you can be sure that when you look at the horses on Cafesjian's Carousel today, most of what you see is the original paint applied by PTC's Gustav Weiss in 1914. There are exceptions, of course, but you aren't likely to detect most of them. Scratched and worn areas have been carefully touched up with paint that matches the original. A handful of horses damaged in the 1939 fire have been newly repainted, after we painstakingly searched for, and found, evidence of their original color schemes.

We know of only one other antique carousel that has been restored to original paint *and* is operated as a ride for the public (PTC6 in Burlington, Colorado). Why are we so lucky? First, the paint on Cafesjian's Carousel survived better than most because for 75 years it ran only for the duration of the Minnesota State Fair—six days to start, gradually increasing to 12. And second, while few carousel operators could afford the time and trouble of restoring and maintaining original paint (even if they had the expertise to do so) Cafesjian's Carousel has enjoyed three special resources: Volunteers, who patiently removed layers of old varnish and park paint; Linda McDonald, whose artistry returned the carousel to its historic beauty; and Jerry Cafesjian, who supported the work with yet another generous gift.

To begin the horse restoration process, we brought in consultant Rosa Ragan of North Carolina, best known for her work on the beautiful Dentzel carousel at Glen Echo Park in Maryland. Rosa did an assessment of each of our horses, carefully recording what she found in order to both guide and record our work. Then she trained a group of volunteers in philosophy and techniques of original-paint restoration.

We wanted to let people see as much of the original paint as possible, but we were also committed to protect that original paint. That meant on most horses we would remove the darkened varnish and any paint that was not original, taking care not to damage the underlying original paint. When the surface was ready, we would seal up the original paint with a protective clear barrier coat. Only then would we touch up the scratches and worn areas, a process known as inpainting.

We had rented a studio in the Lowertown section of downtown Saint Paul and rigged it with a system of tubes and blowers to capture fumes and vent them outside, above the roof of the building. We donned high-performance filtering masks, Tyvek suits, and special nitrile gloves, because we would be disturbing lead-based paint and using strong chemicals. With Rosa coaching us, we explored ways to remove varnish and paint, beginning with the least toxic approach and moving to stronger materials as needed. First we tried hair dryers to soften the varnish, but it was immediately clear that heat alone would not do the job. We tried rubbing alcohol, again with little success. Eventually we landed on an effective though toxic combination of xylene and dimethylformamide, or dmf. We learned to paint it on a patch, maybe two inches square, set a timer for 30 seconds to a minute (depending on the stuff we were removing), wipe the area with cotton balls soaked in mineral spirits to stop the reaction, and then use X-acto knives and dental tools to scrape away the residue (which went into a sealed waste container and then to an approved hazardous waste disposal site). From the beginning, we were very careful to use as few chemicals and generate as little hazardous waste as possible. After restoring 68 horses and two chariots, we had generated only two 55-gallon drums of waste plus 10 gallons of dirty liquid solvents.

Imagine how many square inches there are on 68 horses and two chariots, and then consider that sometimes the same patch had to be done more than once. Volunteers put in hundreds of hours at the studio, clearing away discolored varnish and colors that did not belong. Some time around 1949, new owner Bill Brede's painters had "brightened up" the horses with swashes of black, green, silver, and red on saddles, bridles, hoofs, and tongues. Some of these colors came off relatively easily for us, and others were devilishly stubborn. Leaning over the work usually meant an aching back at the end of a shift. But there was great satisfaction in slowly revealing the delicate colors and patterns Gus Weiss had created.

Linda McDonald's artistic skills had come to the fore during the creation of the paintings for the rounding boards, and she had stepped into a leadership role with the other artists. Now in the restoration studio her skills were again evident. We asked her to supervise the other volunteers and to take charge of the inpainting. Painstakingly mixing colors to match the originals, she expertly disguised scratches and restored color to worn areas. She applied gold and silver leaf wherever she found traces of them, sometimes adding a color glaze. When she was finished, we protected the restored horse with a new coat of varnish, of a type that would not yellow with age.

As we placed the first restored horse back on the inside row, we held a little celebration (covered by three television stations and both daily papers). In contrast to the brown steeds all around it — and in contrast to its appearance months earlier — this horse was a beautiful dapple gray, wearing pink, blue, and gold trappings adorned with branches of silver leaves. We hoped riders would begin to notice and appreciate the transformation. For the next several years, there were always three or four horses missing from the carousel while they went into the studio for restoration. We saved for last the outside row and the horses that had been badly fire-damaged. The charred horses had been repainted after the fire, but we were able to discover their original colors by uncovering original paint still remaining on the left side of the horse, the side away from the fire.

Before long we realized that we needed more of Linda's time than she could give as a volunteer, so with Jerry Cafesjian's help we hired her for the duration of the project. She became a premier restoration artist. Restoration of the horses was completed just before the carousel's grand opening event at Como Park. As Peter told the crowd that evening, "Credit for the beautiful paint on the horses goes first to Gustav Weiss, a German immigrant who worked in Philadelphia in 1914. Credit for restoring the long-lost beauty of that paint goes to Linda McDonald." Now 24 years after she first applied a green stencil pattern to the sweeps and spreaders, Linda continues to maintain the carousel's appearance, touching up paint and leaf that become scratched or worn. She is a member of OFC's board of directors, and during our first season at Como Park she served as the organization's executive director. For the last several years, Linda has sustained her involvement while commuting to Minnesota from Texas. That is dedication.

While we were restoring the horses, we also repaired broken wooden parts according to a carefully defined protocol. Our goal with wood repair was not to make the carousel look new. We chose to leave alone worn spots that we judged to result from ordinary use — carved flowers that had lost their sharp edges, for example, or a cherub's nose rubbed almost flat. On the other hand, we would repair things broken or damaged by something other than simple use. We resolved not to replace original wood unless it was absolutely necessary, and we vowed to be careful not to damage original paint in the course of repairing the wood.

Most of the wood repair was done by volunteer Dick Kenfield, as fine a craftsman as you could ever find. When Dick decided to learn to play the banjo, he first built himself a banjo. When he became interested in Navajo rugs, he went to a reservation, learned how to weave them, and then built his own loom. Dick was a master at sorting out what had caused a break and what would be the best way to repair it. He took a minimalist approach, carefully conserving the original wood and paint wherever possible, respecting the work of the original carvers and painter.

We had designated the pinto pony to be the last horse restored, and Dick was looking forward to it, but he died suddenly, before he was able to begin the work. We remember him with great appreciation for his craftsmanship, and for the kind man he was. He understood perfectly the balance between preservation of the carousel and enjoyment of it. He knew that a person stepping on a horse's leg to mount or dismount might break the leg, and like all our volunteers he and his wife Lorraine were careful to caution people to use the metal step instead. But his focus was always on people, and on keeping the carousel a happy place. Yes, he said one day, it's good to have rules to keep people and horses safe. But enforce them with a smile. The horses are wood; we can fix them.

Our restoration work benefited from expert guidance in the person of Bob Herskovitz, chief objects conservator for the Minnesota Historical Society. Specializing in the care of objects still in use, he taught us, among other things, to search for the right materials in every repair situation. For example, some of our horses had been broken at the knee multiple times over the years, and in a couple of cases the repair had caused even greater damage. When an epoxy used to join two pieces of wood was much stronger than the wood itself, the next time the knee gave way the glue held while the break took a new route through previously undamaged wood. Bob taught us that if something breaks a second time, you want it to break along the original fracture line, and he experimented to find a glue strong enough to hold the joint, but not stronger than the wood. In recent years Linda McDonald, too, has been experimenting to find paints, foil leaf, and coatings that can better stand up to regular use as well as environmental conditions including air pollution.

As we completed the restoration, we left a few glimpses into the past. On two of the burned horses that had to be fully repainted, we left windows in the new paint that show the blackened wood underneath. Where a leg had been braced with an Ovaltine can, we fully repaired the leg but put the can back in place in a tribute to that clever repair. All of the restoration work has been carefully documented so that if, or when, it needs to be done again, workers will know what is original and exactly what we have added. Cafesjian's Carousel, at age 100, enjoys the best of both worlds. It has undergone a museum-quality restoration *and* it is still very much a working carousel.

8

Who Will Write the Next Chapter?

People often comment that Cafesjian's Carousel and its pavilion look perfectly at home in Como Park, as if it had always been there. We're always happy to hear that; the building was designed with that in mind. But we like to remind people that the carousel wasn't always so secure, that it took an enormous community effort to keep it alive and well, and that even now, the carousel depends on the community.

In 1999, as volunteers helped assemble the carousel in its new $1.1 million Victorian pavilion at Como, we all shared a healthy sense of optimism. The park drew good crowds, and plans were underway for new attractions and amenities that would keep people coming and make their stay more pleasant. In the 15 years that Cafesjian's Carousel has operated there, Como Park has added, among other things, a polar bears exhibit, a tropical habitat, and two features that our guests especially appreciate: shuttle service from a remote parking lot and a visitor's center with lots of bathrooms.

We liked the fact that our pavilion would be next to the Marjorie McNeely Conservatory, which was built the year after the carousel and had very recently been restored. Our building felt roomy and functional, with a wider path around the carousel than we'd had downtown, a combined gift shop and ticket sales area, and private space for office, storage, studio, and volunteer areas. Two patio gardens, landscaped and maintained by Como Park staff, provide comfortable seating for folks who like to sit and watch the carousel turn. Even when the building is closed, people can see the carousel year-around through eight large garage doors fitted floor to ceiling with acrylic windows.

Cafesjian's Carousel opened at Como Park on April 15, 2000, a stinging cold and wet day that reminded us that weather would always be a factor in managing the carousel. Too cold, too wet, or too hot, any of these conditions can keep riders away and make life uncomfortable for hard-working volunteers. British millwright Derek Ogden, whose world-class expertise we had sought, advised us never to run the carousel when the temperature is below 45 degrees; the very old cast iron gears could crystallize and fail. We quickly learned that volunteers' hands and faces don't work too well in cold and wind, either. On the other hand, it's a struggle to work on the ride in extreme heat and humidity. So we are weather-watchers; the carousel does not operate when the temperature is below 45 degrees or above 95 degrees. Our season is May 1 through October 31, though Minnesota weather often claims a few days at the beginning or end and sometimes a few in the middle. Thus our climate provides a natural built-in balance, welcoming riders for about half the year and then closing our doors and, we hope, extending the carousel's useful life for the benefit of future generations.

To help us tell the carousel's history, six lighted display panels inside the pavilion feature photos and information, and two display windows accommodate antique carousel figures. As we write this, one window features the rocking horse carved by David Lightfoot for Austin McFadden's son, on loan from the McFadden family. Visitors often stop to read the information cards, look at the rocking horse's head, and turn to find the matching heads on the carousel. The other window, as part of our 100th Birthday season, features menagerie figures on loan from the estate of Jerry Cafesjian.

We dedicated the new building with a ceremony on June 3, 2000. Vic Wittgenstein, who in his role with the Parks and Recreation Department had managed to keep the city and OFC working together through even the most difficult negotiations, was master of ceremonies. When Peter spoke, he began by saluting Vic, a valuable resource from the earliest days of the project. "Vic is a 'civil servant,"' Peter said, "and his *civility* is the reason we are here today." When negotiations got difficult, Vic had the knack for finding common ground. "I would focus on how far apart we were. Vic could always show me the areas where we were close," Peter told the crowd. "When you ride the carousel today, think of Vic. His civility and his knack for finding compromise brought us here."

Jerry Cafesjian and Mayor Norm Coleman together unveiled the sign on the front of the building, and then the people who had adopted horses were ushered in for the first ride of the evening.

The pavilion was built with contributions from the City of Saint Paul, Ramsey County, Jerry Cafesjian, and Our Fair Carousel. (By agreement, the city now owns the building and OFC is halfway through a 30-year renewable lease.) Ramsey County commissioner Janice Rettman, a particular fan of the carousel, proposed that in exchange for the county's $100,000 contribution, we provide free rides to Ramsey County residents five days each summer. Taking things a step further, we now open one Monday each month (we are otherwise closed Mondays for maintenance) and give free rides to all comers. Free Mondays became our first way to thank and serve the community. Another form of service began soon after, and it is especially close to our family's hearts.

In 2001 our daughter Abby's best friend Karen Wyckoff, at age 25, had been battling sarcoma for several years. Karen was looking for a way to raise money and awareness to fight this rare and often-misdiagnosed form of cancer. "I can't run," Karen said, "but

I can ride the carousel. Can we create an event?" We quickly agreed to give free carousel rides for the evening, while Karen's friends and family rounded up musicians, face painters, and other entertainment. Karen died weeks after that modest first event, which has grown to a huge "Party in the Park" raising significant funds each year in late July. The Karen Wyckoff Rein in Sarcoma Foundation now annually awards grants for sarcoma research; it also educates doctors to be alert to signs of sarcoma and provides support for patients and families. Like Our Fair Carousel, the Rein in Sarcoma project was born at a family's kitchen table.

The Arc Greater Twin Cities also started humbly back in 1946 when a parent at a school holiday party suggested working together for the benefit of mentally handicapped children. Arc has grown into a metro-wide organization that advocates public policy and provides direct services, and it was renting the carousel every summer as part of an event to thank volunteers. We now provide the carousel free of charge for them. We remain on the lookout for another partnership through which the carousel, and its volunteers, can help another local charity reach goals important to its mission.

Meanwhile, though, we have been thinking about the well-being of our own organization, and of the carousel it exists to preserve and operate. We estimate that in 74 years under previous owners at the fair the carousel gave roughly 2 million rides. Under our management since 1989, it has given just under 2 million rides. We hope it will be around to give 10 million more. To do that, Cafesjian's Carousel will need to operate successfully enough to pay the bills and keep it from harm. The carousel was rescued, but it is not forever saved.

When we moved the carousel to Como Park, Our Fair Carousel took out a new bank loan for $400,000. With that we paid off our old debt to the city, paid for our share of the pavilion, and covered the costs of moving and assembling the carousel. In November 2005, we made the final payment on that loan, out of carousel revenues and new Adopt-A-Pony donations. It had been 17 years since the two of us, on behalf of OFC, had headed to the

Guernsey's auction with a letter of credit for $1.3 million. Now for the first time, OFC was debt-free. We splurged with a few long-deferred expenditures: a better cash register, a repainted fence, an end-of-season dinner for volunteers.

But an antique carousel has heavy ongoing expenses including insurance premiums, security, maintenance, staffing, and building rent. Earned revenue is limited to what people are willing to pay for a four-minute ride and maybe some mementoes. So we budget conservatively, knowing that weather, nearby construction, the economy, parking, and any number of other factors impact how many people come to ride, and whether they buy something at the gift shop. In 15 years at Como Park we've balanced the budget every year except 2012, when we took in a bit less than we spent. We raised the ticket price the next season — the first time since 1990 — and returned to a balanced budget.

Bigger factors could impact the carousel. Nobody manufactures center bevel gears any more, for example, and if ours failed it would not only be expensive to replace but could keep the carousel shut down for most of a season. A public health crisis that threatens people or zoo animals could force the park to close for an extended period. To protect the carousel in case of such an emergency, and to provide for significant paint restoration in the future, the board is committed to building a half-million-dollar long-term reserve fund. Our best hope for meeting that goal is to find donors who will adopt the remaining horses under our Adopt-A-Pony program. We began in 1988 with 68 horses, two chariots, and a band organ available to be adopted with gifts from $5,000 to $25,000. At this writing, 17 horses and one chariot remain. We hoped to complete the adoptions, and thus the fund, by the carousel's 100th birthday in 2014. Clearly it will take a bit longer.

But the currency most in need is people and their talents — the time, efforts, skills, wisdom, passion, and leadership of people who will keep the carousel turning. Operating an antique carousel — keeping it smooth-running and beautiful, providing a good experience for the rider — is a labor-intensive activity that requires volunteers, staff, and organizational leaders. A list on display at the carousel includes more than 1,000 people who have helped in some way, and we add names every year.

When the carousel became the focus of a major rescue effort, it was just reaching age 75. Now as we celebrate its 100th birthday it is in better condition than ever, rejuvenated by careful attention to the mechanism and restoration of the horses and frame. It is housed in a jewel of a building. But the people involved in that work from the beginning are also 25 years older now. While we may be young at heart, most of us are feeling the effects of advancing age. Our major benefactor has died, as have some of the volunteer colleagues from whom we took heart. For some time now, those who were most involved have been moving on to other things — tending grandchildren, living in a warmer climate, pursuing interests that require less physical activity, for example. There are plenty of opportunities for new volunteers.

It takes five volunteers to staff the carousel when it's open — three on the ride, one selling tickets, and one in the gift shop. With more than 1,300 volunteer shifts per season, we count on our volunteers to contribute more than 4,300 hours every year. They love the carousel; they are dedicated and reliable. The past few years, they have filled nearly every slot. We'd like to have a few more to share the work, but as Peter reminds them at our annual recognition dinner, our absentee rate of 0.5 percent would be the envy of any employer. (Their love of carousels isn't limited to PTC33; every September about 20 of them spend three days visiting carousels in other parts of the country as part of the National Carousel Association convention.)

In the early years, many board members took on other kinds of large-scale volunteer roles — running the gift shop, doing legal work, handling personnel matters, managing wood repair, restoring horses, rebuilding and maintaining the band organ, maintaining the carousel. Jim Weichert has served as our accountant for 25 years. During our first season at Como Park Lorraine Kenfield came in nearly every day to manage the gift shop and to recruit, train, and schedule volunteers. A few others continue in such roles, as we do. But the day will come soon when we step back and others will be needed to provide organizational leadership and participate in everything from fund-raising and communications to keeping the financial books to mixing solvents and responding to middle-of-the-night emergency calls from the security company (so far it's always a false alarm or a malfunction of the sprinkler system due to extreme cold weather, but the firefighters respond and so does Peter). There are new possibilities to explore, like starting a Friends of the Carousel group or doing more cross-promotion with other Como Park attractions, things we haven't had time to pursue.

Just as we didn't foresee how much work we would put into the carousel project over the years, we didn't until recently understand what it would take to replace ourselves in terms of management functions. Unless the carousel again faces imminent danger, nobody is likely to take on as much volunteer responsibility or give up as much personal time as we and the original board have done. And that's okay, as long as we find another approach. In addition to our operations manager Tammi Beckley and our long-time mechanic Mark Carlson, OFC already pays part-time staff to do some of the work once done by volunteers, and it seems inevitable that this trend will expand. What is the right mix of volunteer and staff roles for the future? The right balance of board and staff leadership? How do we afford the more expensive options? These are questions soon to be faced by OFC. Clearly, a new mix of people will be writing the next chapter of the carousel's story.

After 75 years at the state fair, Cafesjian's Carousel is refurbished and sparkling in a pavilion at Como Park. People tell us how happy they are that the carousel is here, where their family will be able to enjoy it in years to come. But wait! Doesn't that sound familiar? Remember when so many of us thought the carousel would always be at the fair?

With your help, it will be around for a long time. Will you help write the next chapter?